Original Strength

Regaining The Body You Were Meant To Have

by

Tim Anderson

and

Geoff Neupert

Table of Contents

Thank You

From Tim:

I cannot thank God enough. He answered a prayer and taught me all that I know. He has blessed me with the information in this book and I am forever grateful.

To my friend Geoff Neupert, thank you. You have been a rock and a great friend. Thank you for your friendship, your ear and your support.

To Mike McNiff, thank you brother. You truly are bulletproof.

To my wife, Addie: You're amazing. Your superhero-like powers of patience will one day be legendary. Thank you for standing by me and listening to all my crazy ideas. I love you.

From Geoff:

Father, thank you! Without you, none of this would've been possible - I would've missed it all!

Tim, what can I say, you are Superman. Thanks for being my brother. Courtney, my wife, thanks for putting up with my craziness. I love you.

Connie, Becker, Elliot, Aron, Minta, Bev, Lee, Eileen, Gary, Peter, and Marel: Thanks for the extreme privilege of working together all these years. You have been my "lab" and my "guinea pigs" and I thank you for trusting me to "test" out my theories. I'm glad this last one was the last one we'll ever need. I will miss you all dearly.

We would both like to thank the outstanding professionals who helped us see "outside the box:" Carla Hannaford and Sally Goddard Blythe and their outstanding work with children, reflexes, and movement. You gave us "eyes to see" what was missing in our field.

Disclaimer!

*Y*ou must get your physician's approval before beginning this exercise program.

These recommendations are not medical guidelines but are for educational purposes only. You must consult your physician prior to starting this program or if you have any medical condition or injury that contraindicates physical activity. This program is designed for healthy individuals 18 years and older only.

See your physician before starting any exercise or nutrition program. If you are taking any medications, you must talk to your physician before starting any exercise program, including the *Original Strength* program. If you experience any lightheadedness, dizziness, or shortness of breath while exercising, stop the movement and consult a physician.

It is strongly recommended that have a complete physical examination if you are sedentary, if you have high cholesterol, high blood pressure, or diabetes, if you are overweight, or if you are over 30 years old. Please discuss all nutritional changes with your physician or a registered dietician. If your physician recommends that you not use the *Original Strength* program, please follow your Doctor's orders.

All forms of exercise pose some inherent risks. The authors, editors, and publishers advise readers to take full responsibility for their safety and know their limits. Before practicing the exercises in this exercise program, and do not take risks beyond your level of experience, aptitude, training and fitness. The exercises and dietary programs in this program are not intended as a substitute for any exercise routine or treatment or dietary regimen that may have been prescribed by your physician.

Foreword

*I*n June of 2009 I signed up for a specialty training certification called the Russian Kettlebell Challenge (RKC). At this time the RKC was considered the authority on professional Kettlebell instruction and strength enhancement principles. When I arrived, I found myself placed onto a team of 12, with our lead instructor a person I had never heard of before named Geoff Neupert. I was feeling like I was going to have an average experience at best, since my primary instructor was not someone I had ever heard of in the industry. More on this in a moment, but first a little more background on how I ended up here in the first place is needed.

Up to this point in 2009 I had been in the strength and conditioning industry working as a strength coach, performance enhancement specialist, and personal trainer since 1996. As I was developing as a professional over those 13 years, I was fortunate enough to have the opportunity to meet and be educated and mentored by several leading experts within the industry. Incredibly intelligent, highly educated, and experienced professionals like Mike Boyle, Mark Verstegen and Gray Cook formed my education and expertise, and helped me develop my brand and system of professional performance enhancement training.

When Gray Cook introduced me to the Kettlebell in the summer of 2008, I immediately saw the movement and performance benefits the tool provided, unlike other tools, through its unique design and specific utilization. However, I was resistant to the idea of attending a certification like the RKC based on, what I thought at the time, was a certification simply geared around a specific tool. In addition it appeared on the surface that the RKC didn't have any industry leading experts that could teach me much about movement or performance enhancement. After all, they had a lot to measure up to in my mind since I had spent my entire career learning from the masters of movement and performance like Gray, Mark and Mike! So what exactly could a fringe specialty group like the RKC and some guy named Geoff Neupert really teach someone like me who had been seasoned for 13 years in the performance enhancement industry? I actually said this to Gray and he smiled in a way that let me know I didn't really have a full understanding of what I was missing. He told me to simply trust him and attend a RKC. He persuaded me that it would be well worth my time and money, with a simple "trust me".

I was still skeptical of the whole RKC thing, but with Gray's endorsement I decided to take his word for it and attend one. I figured at worst I would learn a little more about the kettlebell even if I didn't have top-level industry experts instructing me. Oh, how little did I realize!

Back to my RKC in 2009 and my "no name" team instructor Geoff Neupert. I had walked in assuming after years of education from the Gray Cook's and Mark Verstegen's of the world that there was no possible way some guy I had never even heard of named Geoff Neupert was going to be able to further my education or impress me in any way. I mean he didn't even know how to spell his own name correctly. I figured based on this alone the weekend would be a complete wash.

I couldn't have been more wrong. I mean way, way stupid wrong! Geoff (aka Jeff) was simply an incredible instructor. He knew as much about movement, the body, how it works, performance enhancement, and how the Kettlebell, applied properly, can enhance and improve all of those things, as anyone I had ever met and learned from in all my 13 years in the industry. I was thoroughly impressed with Geoff's expertise and command of not only the kettlebell, but also his command of the principles and concepts of movement and performance enhancement. In fact to this day when we speak and talk shop I'm always thoroughly impressed at how in command and precise he is with his knowledge. He has a way of saying things that's so clear and concise, yet so simple, a true expert and master. I used to think the title "master" was kind of dumb in the Kettlebell world. Then I met a couple of them (like Geoff) and now I think it's totally appropriate.

My RKC course was one of the best and most influential educational experiences in my career to date. Geoff was the primary reason. I was amazed at how intelligent he was on strength and conditioning principles, performance enhancement concepts and on how to apply various methods to training to get maximum results and optimal outcomes for clients and athletes. I simply could not believe how much of an industry expert this guy actually was, right in line with the people I held in my mind at the top of the field.

I left my RKC with a new respect for the organization and especially for Geoff. In a weekend he had gone from a guy I had never heard of, that I assumed wouldn't be able to teach me much, to a respected mentor and teacher that I would learn from for years to come and continue to learn from even as I write this. That's how smart Geoff is, that's how educated he is. Anytime you can meet a person in three days and instantly they become a mentor, you know you have found someone very special.

That brings me to Tim Anderson. I met Tim recently through Geoff at the workshop they teach together, Becoming Bulletproof. Admittedly, I did not know Tim very well. However you do not need to know Tim for more then a few minutes before you figure out that he is clearly one of the most humble and genuine people you will ever meet. His energy and personality exudes warmth, caring and love. His approach towards people and teaching comes completely out of a place of wanting to share and help in any way he can, truly the embodiment of the word genuine.

Tim is the smartest person in the room that you will never know about because he is simply not interested or worried about if people think he's smart. He's there totally to share his experience and knowledge, and most uniquely, learn all about yours. Many experts cannot hear because they are too busy talking. Tim is all about hearing you, understanding you and then doing whatever he can to help you, if you like. He demonstrates a truly impressive, highly effective approach to teaching that only the best at their craft execute naturally. Tim is masterful at seeking to understand you and then finding a way to take his knowledge and help you.

I discovered all of this in that one day of meeting and learning from Tim. Tim is the type of person you just want to get to know and have in your life as soon as you meet him. There is "something" about him that just feels good and right. Did I mention he is incredibly smart and a fantastic teacher? The qualities he has that I described above make him the best kind of teacher because he gets you to a place of being completely open so you can fully take in the message of what he is teaching.

Together Geoff and Tim have put their immense education, knowledge, expertise and expert teaching abilities into the truly amazing book you are about to read, Original Strength.

Original Strength is truly groundbreaking information. It takes potentially complex concepts and principles about human movement, development, and performance and explains them in an easy to understand step-by-step format. Geoff and Tim provide an organized systematic approach with Original Strength to help you implement and apply the information being taught to anyone under any circumstances or conditions.

Every drill taught follows and adheres to the principles by which it's built on and each drill has a logical, rational and scientific explanation that outlines the what, why and how. Everything you want to know gets explained, everything makes common sense as well as scientific sense, and everything has been proven to work because it already has once for all of us. If you don't already know what I'm talking about, don't worry, you will right after you read pages 6-12.

I personally work with every type of person from high profile professional athletes to 75 year olds, to stay at home moms, to 13 year olds, to the chronically injured, and everything in between. The Original Strength principles and drills that you will read about and learn are implemented every day at my facility with every type of client and athlete. It's universal to all clients no matter what the goal or situation, because movement and moving well is universal to living a life of vitality and high performance for all human beings, regardless of age, sport or condition. After reading the book you will see how easy it is to find an appropriate level, regression or progression of every concept and drill, for every situation and person you work with.

I have had amazing results with the Original Strength system since its inclusion into my existing system of training. People begin to move free of restriction more so than before, more natural and authentic with better coordination. Movements, exercises or things they could not do before, now they can do much better or for the first time ever in some cases. Strength and performance markers all increase across the board, often with personal records being set or achieved again for the first time in years. Pain levels and injuries significantly improve, and most importantly everyone feels a noticeable change within their own body.

It's clear and evident that Original Strength is affecting you positively. You can't help but notice, and in some cases it's so obvious and somewhat instantaneous that it's quite shocking at first. Some things are more subtle and not everyone has the keen body awareness to notice what you see in them change, but they will definitely notice their knee not hurting as much when they squat, that Kettlebell they are pressing moving overhead 5x instead of 4x, improved coordination and speed dropping under a barbell snatch, being able to balance and squat on one leg where before they kept falling over, or touching their toes for the first time. Original Strength has the ability to bring back to life the foundation of posture, balance and coordination within our bodies giving us freedom to express our true athleticism and strength. And the best part is that it happens the way it was meant to happen, *naturally and authentically,* which means you get to keep it and own it for your life. Just don't lose it again and if you do for whatever reason just go back to Original Strength. It's always there waiting for you to "press reset".

My whole professional career has been about and is about bringing the very best training system and methods possible to my athletes and clients so I can make them the most optimal and highest performing version of themselves. I am honored every day by those individuals that have trusted in me and given me the opportunity to do just that. I want to do my absolute very best work for them every day. For this very reason, for this mission I have, I choose to use Original Strength. Original Strength is some of the very best information that I have ever seen to accomplish what I am committed to for my athletes and clients. If you want to change your life and the lives of those you care about or that have entrusted you with their health, fitness and/or performance then turn the page and let the next step in that process begin. It could be the most important step you will ever take to fulfilling your own personal mission or towards living a more enriched life full of vitality and freedom in your body.

With that, I give you Geoff Neupert and Tim Anderson's Original Strength, a pioneering educational experience from two amazing teachers and people. Regain your movement. Improve your strength. Change your life!

Thank you,

Joe Sansalone, Owner, Optimum Performance Training Institute

Introduction

Your Original Strength

*I*n the beginning, you were created perfectly. When you were born, your brain had a movement template that was "hard wired" into yourself, and your body was a blank slate ready and willing to grow with perfect strength and mobility. You spent your infant and toddler years learning how to move, building strength and completely integrating your whole body. You glued everything about yourself together: your nervous system, vestibular system, visual system, muscular system, proprioceptive system, digestive system - every system you have, you integrated them together. Your body became whole - one cohesive unit. You were one piece called a body; not one body of several pieces and systems.

Through learning how to move, you nourished and developed your brain and you built and developed your body, gaining strength by the day. As you developed, movement and strength became one of the same. You moved with the strength you developed and the strength you developed helped you move. From the beginning, you were meant to move with grace, fluidity and strength. You were meant to conquer life, not be its victim.

When you were a child, you were well on your way to strength and vitality - you held life in your design. You were meant to be strong. In fact, you were strong! Then, something happened, something changed. You no longer explored your world through movement. You stopped using your body. You became stagnant. You became civilized. Now, that childhood has passed away, you intuitively know that something is wrong. You cannot move the way that you wish you could. In your imagination, you remember how strong you were when you were younger and you dream about things you wish you could do, but no longer can because of fear, pain, or lack of health. You toss out phrases like, "when you hit thirty, everything falls apart." Don't resign yourself to those thoughts of defeat. You were young and strong once, and you can be that way again.

The same movement template that was in you as a child, the same reflexes you were wired with, are still inside of you right now. The same perfect strength and grace you once had is still available, and able to be built again. You can regain the strength you were meant to have. You can reclaim the body that is rightfully yours. You do not have to watch life go by on your two cheeks. You can rage against your current state and regain what was always yours to be had - your original strength. You were meant to live a life of vitality. You were meant for more than apathy and lethargy, a life on the sidelines, "living" vicariously through others - that is death pretending to be alive, "life" awaiting death. You were made to be a conqueror, not a survivor - to live and engage.

You need to know this. And, you need to do this: **You need to regain your strength.** There is more to life than aches, pains, lethargy, obesity, high blood pressure, diabetes, and heart disease. *You were not meant for any of these things!* Almost all of life's "issues" could be combated and defeated if we would regain our simple movement patterns and engage in them on a regular basis. No matter what the state of your body is right now, you can go back to the beginning and start regaining your original strength. You can turn back both the hands of time and the neglect of your body.

<u>Everything you need to become resilient and strong is already inside of your brain, waiting to be tapped into.</u>

Do not settle for existence. Stir yourself up and reclaim what was yours from the beginning. **Don't pretend to be alive, come alive!**

Reclaim your strength, your original strength, and enjoy the life you were meant to have - a life of movement exploration: climbing mountains, swimming seas, sprinting through fields, rolling on the ground, or simply playing chase or catch with your children. Those things aren't just supposed to look "cool" in the movies. Those things should be an everyday part of your life! They should be your reality and not your fantasy! You were meant to live, to have vitality.

It is time to engage! Reclaim your birthright and rebuild the strength you once had so you can enjoy this life. You **can** become strong again. You can regain your **original strength.** It is **simple**. All you have to do are the things you once did so well. You just have to become a child again. Not all childish ways were meant to be put away. Learn how to move and build strength again, as a child does, as you once did. Again, **everything** you need to become strong, healthy and resilient is already inside of you right now, and now is the time to engage.

Now is the time to regain your original strength, the strength you were designed to have. Now is the time to explore your world through the eyes and ways of a child.

This book is a continuation and integration of the thoughts and conversations from *Becoming Bulletproof* and *Pressing Reset*. Since the release of those two books, my friend, Geoff Neupert and I have gained even more understanding on how amazing the body is and how well it responds to our original movement template. Much of the information in this book will be a review, but we will also be delving deeper in our presentation to reveal the wonder of how **_simple_** it can be to regain our bodies' original strength

Tim Anderson
Fuquay-Varina, North Carolina,
March 2013

We Are Fearfully
And Wonderfully Made

*T*his is true. The human body is the most awesome creation the world has ever known. It is capable of almost anything. Therefore, YOU are capable of almost anything. You were designed to be without limits - both physically and mentally. This message was, and is, the heart of *Becoming Bulletproof: An Uncommon Approach to Building a Resilient Body*.

The human body was truly made to be resilient. We should be able to run, jump and play without sustaining nagging injuries or acquiring other "movement issues." When we are 70 years old, we should still have a healthy body that allows us to enjoy life; a body free from pain, restrictions, and limitations. The body was designed to grow older, this happens with time. However, the body was not meant to age. At least, the body was not meant to age in the way that we are allowing ourselves to age.

Aging happens with lack of use. Aging is the result of not living and moving the way we were meant to. As we grow older, we should still be able to move around much like we did when we were teenagers, or the way we did when we were in our twenties for those of you who don't think you can move like you did as a teenager.

Think about it. We really are wonderfully made. What would be the point of growing older without vitality? We were meant to live and enjoy this life. We weren't meant to grow older only to lose our independence. That is not growing older, that is aging.

Aging happens to us when we spend our lives being static, when we allow stress and fears to consume us, when all we do is work and not play. Aging is a result of using our bodies, or not using our bodies rather, for something other than what they were intended. We were meant to move, to play, and to engage life. We need to get back to doing these things so we can grow old with vitality.

And we can. We cannot reverse time. We will grow older. But we can reverse the aging process - to a degree. We can regain our vitality. We can enter our 90s with vibrance. We don't have to wonder if we will be bed-ridden by the time we are 70.

Geoff and I have been learning this lesson in our own lives. I am knocking at the door of 40, and Geoff, well, he is already there, but daily we find ourselves engaging in new activities that we could have never done in our twenties. I certainly move better today and have more energy than I did when I was younger, and Geoff is constantly finding that he is able to perform physical tasks better than he was able to fifteen years ago.

So how are we doing this? The answer is ridiculously simple. We are moving with the same movements we used to build strength with as a child. We are engaging in life. And that's great news: We (people) get to have a huge say in how we grow older. We don't have to age. And, if we find ourselves aging, we can make **simple** changes and become vibrant again.

If you want to have a resilient body, if you want to grow old with vitality and you don't want to simply age and exist, start moving like you did when you were a child. It is amazing what a difference this will make in your body. It is so amazing that it is almost a miracle. *Engaging* in "child-like" movements is the key to turning back the hands of time. and reclaiming the body you were meant to have.

Wonderful things happen when children learn to roll, creep, crawl and walk. They build perfectly strong and mobile bodies. They become amazingly resilient. This resiliency is not meant to fade away with time! We should be resilient throughout our entire lives!

Fortunately, the body is so amazing, even as adults, we can regain our original strength, our resiliency, by engaging in the same movements we used to develop our bodies to start with! We can actually regain our vitality by simply spending time on the floor and moving like a child.

Life is meant to be enjoyed. If you really want to be able to enjoy your life, you need a healthy body. Being in pain and always being injured should not be the norm or the status quo. It should not be a result of time simply passing us by! Even in our 70s, we should be able to go for a run without getting knee pain. We should be able to pick up a suitcase without hurting our backs. We should be able to grab something out of the back seat of our car without tearing a rotator cuff. We should be resilient! ***We were not meant to be fragile.***

STOP aging!

You are not supposed to decline with time. Wake up the resilient kid inside of yourself and start moving like you once did. Learn how to press the "reset button" on your body and rebuild the body you were meant to have: A strong, flexible, powerful body capable of climbing any mountain or swimming any sea at **any age.** You are meant to grow old with strength and health, which by default means with grace and dignity, something that so many of us long for, but are scared we may not have. You are meant to be able to wrestle with your grand-kids and go for long walks with your spouse. Growing older should be a wonderful process, not something to be dreaded and feared. Join us, press the "reset" button on your body and regain the body you were always meant to have.

Most of the information that follows in this book has been well researched and applied in the areas of learning disabilities, brain development and brain rehabilitation. We are extrapolating from these ideas used for building a healthy brain and applying this information, along with our own ideas, observations, and experiences, towards building a healthy body. It is the culmination of several peoples' work, from both the fitness and physical therapy fields. Since the writing of *Becoming Bulletproof*, we have had over two years of experiences and hundreds of testimonials to substantiate the information that we are presenting in this book. Two years from now, I know we will continue to be blown away by both what we know to be true, and by what we still have yet to learn.

The human body is indeed fearfully and wonderfully made.

Babies Move To Live

*B*abies, children, develop perfectly through learning how to move. Even before a child sees the light of this world, he starts developing his brain and muscles inside his mother's womb through movement. Once a child is born, the reflexes and movement patterns that are already etched deep into the brain start building an amazing foundation of strength through movement exploration. In turn, this wonderful strength that is being developed through movement actually helps develop the brain and nervous system through the very movements that are creating the strength. In other words, our bodies and brain are developed through a cycle of movement. The more we move through our natural movement patterns, the more we develop our brain. The more we develop our brain, the more efficient we become at moving. The more efficient we become at moving, the better we move, and the more we further develop our brain. This cycle can and should go on and on throughout our entire lives.

In case any of the above paragraph was confusing, here is a summation: When we were children, we learned to move through specific movement patterns that were etched deep inside our brains. As we moved using these patterns, we developed and strengthened both our bodies *and* our brains. Brain development and body development are not mutually exclusive events. They go hand in hand. As one develops, the other is nourished and developed. Learning to move and engaging in movement even develops who we are as individuals. In *The Well Balanced Child,* Ewout Van-Manen points out that *". . .physical movement is the basis for cognitive, social and emotional development."*[1] The body is so amazing! (Which of course means, by default, that lack of cognitive, social, and emotional development can be traced back to a lack of movement.)

The brain and the body nourish and develop each other. However, movement is the catalyst for this nourishment. Movement builds **everything** about you. Through movement, we develop our "body map," our sense of self in space. This is called proprioception.[2] Our body is filled with sensors, and proprioceptors in our skin, joints, tendons, and muscles, that feed our brain with a sense of self every time we move and experience our environment. The more we move, the more we flood our brain with information from our proprioceptors about what our body is doing and where our body is at. This flood of information creates a good "body map", or "movement map" in our brains. The better our body map is, the better we move.

Not only does movement improve your proprioception, it actually *physically changes and improves your brain!* Physical activity develops brain tissue![3] Inside your brain, there are millions of nerve connections, or nerve networks. Movement improves the communication between these connections and actually cements new connections.[4] The better you move, the more efficient your brain becomes. **The more efficient your brain becomes, the better you move.**

Again, brain development and body development go hand in hand. It's a two-way street and movement is the vehicle. Movement is life. It is the key to every facet of our health. It shapes everything about us: Our brains, our bodies, who we are as people, our emotions, our hormones, even our mental health.[5]

We are simply made to move. Yet, most of us don't. Instead we sit. So, we lose our movement patterns, or we replace them with sitting. We slow our brain development. In some ways, our brain development regresses. This process is called neuronal fitness or neuronal pruning.[6] Just as movement can shape and develop our brains, not moving can also shape our brains. Simply put, our brains prune out the nerve connections we don't need or the ones we don't use often. The neural connections in the brain are much like the movement patterns in the body: **Use it or lose it.**

We live in a world filled with technological innovations and conveniences. We have computers, cars, and the internet. There is no need for us to get up and move. If we want to go shopping, we only have to jump online and push a button or two. We don't even have to get out and go to the mall anymore! Every year we grow further and further away from physical bodies capable of anything to bodies capable of being paper weights. We are wonderfully made, yet we don't allow ourselves to participate in the wonder for which we were created. We were made to move, anywhere and everywhere. Yet most of us spend our time going nowhere. We occupy the same square footage of a chair for hours and hours every day. Many kids today are not even learning how to run, how to skip, or how to climb. We are moving further and further away from what we were made for: movement. Remember, movement is life, ***and_life is movement!***

There are some things we cannot change. Kids have to go to school, adults have to go to work. In today's world we are going to spend a lot of time sitting. However, that doesn't mean we can't learn to minimize the time we spend sitting, and it doesn't mean we can't keep our bodies fit and capable of doing anything. We can learn to move deliberately. We can regain our movement patterns and rid ourselves of our movement limitations. **We can become healthy and resilient again. We can regain our original strength!**

You need to know this. In our lifetimes, we are not meant to have only a "season" of health. The body is far too amazing for such a season. We are meant to live a "life" of health. Yes, we will grow older, but we do not have to age and decay. We were not made to be strong and healthy for the first twenty to thirty years of our lives only to grow weak, injured, or decrepit for the last forty to sixty years of our lives. We are designed to be strong, resilient and physically capable of anything throughout our entire lives!

The strength we once had can be ours again. All we have to do is learn how to move in the ways in which we once did. To do this, we only need to look at how children grow and develop. Babies move to live. They build a foundation of strength through reflexes and movement patterns that are deeply rooted in their brains. From these reflexes and movement patterns, they then learn to move in all possible combinations of movements and in all planes of motion. Their movement exploration builds strong, healthy, resilient bodies. Bodies that are meant to last a lifetime.

X Marks The Spot!

*T*he road, or the map, to regaining our original strength revolves around the center of the X. The X is you. And the center of your X and you is your midsection, your abs, your core. And having a reflexively strong and solid center is the key to regaining our original strength. Without a solid center, we will never be able to be as strong as we should be. Please note, a reflexively strong center is not something you can get from doing traditional abdominal exercises. It is earned and obtained by engaging in your original movement patterns and the reflexes that they stimulate and sharpen. A solid center is developed by global input from the entire body: Diaphragmatic breathing, movement patterns, reflexes, vestibular information (balance system input), proprioceptive information (sensory nerves), brain development - all of these and more contribute to building a powerful center, thus producing a powerful body.

Understand this: *We are fully integrated.* Everything about you works together to make your whole body powerful and strong. If we were to remove any one facet of our body, like wearing thick soled shoes all of our lives, or if we tried to isolate one of our body's systems from another, we will weaken the entire body. A child develops an amazingly strong body by exploring movement and fully integrating movement with his or her senses and systems. An adult can do the same thing! We can recapture our strong centers, we can rebuild our X, by engaging in and exploring the same movements we did as a developing child.

Like we mentioned earlier, you are the X. That is, the body is an X. Not only are we shaped like one big X, but our entire body is made up of a series of Xs. Just look at an anatomy chart of muscles and notice how the muscles and tendons lie in relation to one another. Even our DNA is in the shape of a double helix, a spiraling X. We are literally a series of connected Xs from head to toe. In order for us to be as strong and resilient as we were meant to be, the center of our X has to be knit together properly; much like a tightly woven Chinese finger trap. The center of our X, our core, is where the forces we generate from movement cross over from one side of our body to the other. These forces cross through our center from left to right, right to left, bottom to top, and top to bottom. The more "connected" our X is, the more efficient the forces can cross over. We are made to be efficient and powerful.

It may help to think of your center, the center of your X, as ranging from your pelvic floor to your armpits with your belly button being in the dead center. However you think of the core, it is the crossroads of force production. When everything is working as it should, the core is the crossroads of efficient and powerful forces; the key to a strong and resilient body.[7] When things in the core are not functioning properly, the core can be the crossroads of energy chaos; forces end up going in areas they shouldn't, creating unnecessary stresses, energy leakages, and movement dysfunctions. In other words, if your center, or your core, is not functioning properly, you will not be as powerful as you were meant to be, and you may be at a higher risk of injury as well as a myriad of other issues like poor digestion, unbalanced hormones, sluggish metabolism and so on. . .

Remember, our bodies are fully integrated. Your X is knit together by everything about you. Your vestibular system, or your balance system, is tied to your core. [8] Your grip is tied to your core. Your feet are tied to your core. Your skin is tied to your core. Your emotions are even tied to your core. Your core is tied to **EVERYTHING**. It all works together. Nothing is isolated. **Everything is integrated**.

Unfortunately, we are really good at isolating things that should not be isolated. We create conveniences in life that allow us to be comfortable so we don't have to move. Things like chairs, rear view mirrors, computers, remote controls, etc. We have gotten really good at not moving our heads or our bodies. We have become masters of disintegration. In return, we lose some of our movement patterns, we stagnate our vestibular system, we lose our reflexively stable core, and we become broken. We lose these things not simply because we do not use them but because we do not need them with our current lifestyles.

It is time to knit our centers back together again, and regain our original strength, the strength we once had as a child. If we really want to become physically resilient and strong, we need to do what babies do. We need to regain our strength and mobility through movement - very particular movements we will discuss soon.

But, before we dive into these movements, we need to go over the three rules to regaining our original strength:

1. You have to know how to breathe.

2. You have to stimulate your vestibular system.

3. You have to cross midline and/or engage in your contra-lateral patterns.

If we do these three things, we will be as strong and healthy as we could ever want to be, as we were meant to be.

Just Breathe

$\mathcal{B}$reathing properly is vital to regaining our original strength. If you are not breathing properly, learning how to breathe could be the most important concept in this whole book for you. Breathing is perhaps the most overlooked, undervalued, and most critical reflex you possess. When a child is born, the first real reflex and movement they engage in is breathing. Babies breathe correctly right from the start: They use their diaphragms. Babies don't breathe high up in the chest like most adults do. Instead, they pull air down deep into their lungs with their diaphragm and by doing so, they are strengthening the center of their X. In other words, breathing is and should be core training - strength training for your core. For some reason, adults unlearn, or retrain, this natural breathing reflex. And in doing so, we weaken our core, the center of our X. Just relearning and regaining our natural way of breathing can be the greatest step we ever take towards regaining our original strength. In fact, it may be impossible to unlock your full strength and health potential without breathing properly. All your attempts to become healthy and resilient will just be stacked up on a faulty breathing pattern, a pattern that will only strengthen weakness and stress.

Just in case you don't remember, when you were born, you were a diaphragmatic breather, or a "belly" breather. You were born this way for a reason. Just watch any new born baby, or infant. You will see their little bellies go up and down when they breathe. They are taking full advantage of their lung volume by effortlessly breathing with their diaphragm (let's call that our "breathing muscle"). The diaphragm pulls a vacuum in the lungs allowing them to fill themselves full of life-giving air. The diaphragm, also massages the internal organs thus aiding in digestion. And, perhaps most importantly, the diaphragm works with the pelvic floor to help create a reflexively stable core. It may help to imagine that the diaphragm and the pelvic floor both work together to form a "box of strength" in your center. Remember, the more solid your center is, the more strength, power, speed, and resilience you will possess.

Again, this is how we are born breathing - with our diaphragm. Some of us, or most of us, end up retraining how we breathe by using our accessory muscles, or the muscles in our rib cage, neck and shoulders. These are the muscles a baby uses to breathe when his breathing is compromised and he is in distress. When babies use these muscles to breathe, they are usually sick and may need emergency medical attention. It may help to think of these accessory breathing muscles as *emergency breathing muscles.*

For some reason, whether it is due to our stressful lives, or because we are trying to hide our gut, we become "chest breathers," and we start using our accessory respiratory muscles to breathe.

Remember, the accessory respiratory muscles are our "emergency" breathing muscles. We really don't need to be using these all the time. They are our startle, or fight or flight, muscles.

> ### What Is Reflexive Stability?
>
> Reflexive Stability is your body's subconscious ability to anticipate movement before it actually move and prepare the joints and muscles involved in that movement for that movement. More on this later. . .

Constantly breathing with our emergency muscles can cause a forward head carriage, neck pain, poor thoracic mobility, hunched forward posture, early fatigue when exercising, poor digestion, **and** a loss of our reflexive stability in our core muscles. If we are always breathing with our emergency breathing muscles, our bodies are always in stress mode, which is a very inefficient, unhealthy mode to be stuck in for a long period of time. Some people spend a lifetime breathing like this.

The good news is if we can change our breathing pattern for the bad, then we can also retrain our breathing pattern for the good. Breathing is a natural reflex that is subconscious (like all reflexes). However, breathing can also be controlled and trained consciously. In *Becoming Bulletproof*, we introduced crocodile breathing as a way to relearn how to diaphragmatically breathe. In crocodile breathing, you lay on your belly and rest your forehead on the back of your hands. While inhaling through your nose, you want to try to breathe deep down into your belly. If you do this correctly, your belly will push against the floor and cause your lower back to rise up. The sides of your belly will also get wider, just like a crocodile! This can be a very effective way to retrain yourself how to become a belly breather. It is not the only way though.

There are many ways in which one can practice belly breathing. (We cover a series of breathing "regressions" in our workshops that help many people "discover" the magic of breathing and its correlation to better movement and performance.) Perhaps the most effective way is to just spend time on the floor like a child and deliberately try to breathe deep into your belly while you explore different positions. You may need to rest your hands on your belly to increase awareness of your desired target, or imagine you are trying to breathe all the way through the bottom of your feet to encourage deep breaths. It doesn't matter how you do it, as long as you can do it - effortlessly, in any position.

Learning how to breathe properly can unlock a whole host of health benefits and really lay the foundation for regaining your original strength. If you train with weights or if you lift heavy objects, using your diaphragm when you breathe allows you to create more intra-abdominal pressure.[9] That is to say, you can brace your body better to pick up a heavy load. It is kind of like *zipping up a girdle around your midsection*. Not only is this good for you, it could save you from a career ending injury!

Being a belly breather will allow you to be more efficient in your day to day activities, as well as your sport of choice. This is because you are able to take in more air, and you are not using as much energy by breathing with your accessory muscles. People that constantly breathe using their emergency muscles often carry a great deal of tension and "tightness" throughout their neck and shoulders. This tension is can be seen as a constant muscular contraction. Muscles require energy to contract. Constantly using your accessory muscles to breathe has a metabolic cost; you tire more quickly.

Being a belly breather may be one way to keep and/or regain a reflexively stable core. This is very important in day to day life because as we discussed earlier when talking about how the body is an X, a reflexively stable core transfers forces from the ground through the torso efficiently. In other words, a reflexively stable core is crucial for health because it yields a strong and stable body. If you do not have a reflexively strong center, your body will not be strong, and you will be more likely to get injured. Diaphragmatic breathing, belly breathing like a child, can be one of the best exercises you could ever do to regain your original strength.

Now that we've taken a look at diaphragmatic breathing, perhaps the most important reflex we possess for overall health and resiliency, let's look at the most important system in the body: *The vestibular system.*

The Vestibular System

A healthy vestibular system is necessary for a healthy, strong body. In fact, total health cannot exist separate from a healthy vestibular system. The vestibular system, your balance system, is perhaps the most important sensory system you have. Everything about you is shaped by how your vestibular system functions: Your sense of self your reality, your balance, your posture, your ability to hold your head up and maintain your gaze with the horizon, your ability to learn, your experiences, everything.[10] You can function without other sensory systems and lead a somewhat "normal" life. For instance, a blind man can learn to be independent and get around almost as well as people who have sight. But a person who's vestibular system is out of whack may not be able to have a "normal" life. Just ask anyone who has ever had vertigo and they will tell you just how important a healthy vestibular system is for feeling "normal" and healthy.

The vestibular system lives in your head, or your inner ears. It is composed of highly sensitive organs called the utricle, saccule, and semicircular canals.[11] Without getting too scientific, they are like having your own internal gyroscopes inside your head. The organs are filled with tiny hairs and a gel-like substance. When your head moves, the liquid substance moves the tiny hairs and sends information to your brain. Basically, they work to give you equilibrium and balance.[12]

The vestibular system is the **first** system to begin developing in the fetus, inside the womb. It is also the foundation that all other sensory systems are built upon, or routed through, rather. It begins developing about 21 days after conception,[13] and it is fully developed about 5 months after conception.[14] Even in the womb, the mother's movements provide stimulation to the developing vestibular system. This stimulation helps develop the child's nervous system. Once a child is born, the new world of gravity and all the challenges it brings begin to further stimulate the vestibular system and shape the nervous system with the new movements the child begins to make.

As mentioned above, all other sensory systems - ALL systems are routed through the vestibular system. [15] Your proprioceptive system, or your inner sense of self, is intimately tied to your vestibular system.[16] Together, they form your body map, or your movement map. Your visual system is tied to your vestibular system. Ninety percent of the cells in your visual system respond to vestibular information.[17] Your autonomic nervous system (the system that controls the things you don't consciously control like your heart rate, respiratory rate, your digestion, perspiration, arousal, etc. . .) is tied to your vestibular system.[18] The vestibular system is also connected to every single muscle in your body, especially the core and neck muscles![19] Even your emotions can be affected by your vestibular system.[20] Did I mention that everything about your body is tied to your vestibular system? The vestibular system seems to be the foundational system that the rest of "you" is built upon.

Therefore, *a healthy vestibular system is crucial to having a healthy body.* We, you, want a healthy vestibular system! We can strengthen our vestibular system the same way that babies do: *We move!* The more we move, the more we stimulate our vestibular system. The more we stimulate our vestibular system, the more nerve connections we make in our brain and our body. It has even been shown that children who receive regular vestibular stimulation show advanced development in motor skills.[21] Remember, all your muscles are tied to your vestibular system. If we continually stimulate our vestibular system, we continually stimulate all of our muscles in some way, especially our core and neck muscles. Not only that, but the more we stimulate and strengthen our vestibular system, the more we strengthen, or solidify, the health of all of our bodies' other systems.

When we don't move, we are not stimulating the vestibular system. In other words, we are not stimulating the brain, the nervous system, or the muscular system. Think of it this way, everything about the body follows the rule, "use it or lose it." The vestibular system is no different. If we do not train one of our most important senses or systems, perhaps the most important system we have, it will begin to deteriorate much like our calculus skills slip away after we get out of college. Sally Goddard Blythe points out that one of the first signs of brain deterioration is when balance starts to deteriorate.[22] If your vestibular system is indeed connected to every muscle in your body, your ability to move well will also deteriorate when your vestibular system deteriorates.

This is important: **The vestibular system is tied to the core musculature of the abdominals and back,** and it is these muscles that first work together to move the head.[23] The vestibular system is stimulated by neck movement, as well as other things. Moving the neck and head is tied to your core musculature. When a child picks up his head while lying on the floor, he is developing his core, his entire X, and training his vestibular system. They are not mutually exclusive.

Don't miss this: *Learning how to move the head, developing head control, is how a child first starts building real strength.* Mastering head control is essential to balance, posture, and coordination.[24] Read that again: Mastering head control is essential to balance, posture, and coordination. Isn't that simply saying that mastering head control is essential to strength and vitality? Do you want to regain your original strength? You need to master good head control!

It is **our belief** that when we sit all day and keep our heads still without moving our necks, we are detraining and weakening our body. Again, this is our hypothesis, but it makes a ton of sense. (As a side note, we have tested our hypothesis over the last three years on ourselves and with our clients. Our results have found that by using simple head control exercises, our posture is significantly better, and so is the control and functioning of the rest of our bodies, including an increase in strength and reflexes.) The human body is designed to move. Every system, every facet of the body is fully integrated. There is nothing about the body that is mutually exclusive from another part of itself. So, **EVERYTHING** about you is tied together in some way. The secret to obtaining real strength and health could be as simple as learning how to move your head.

To recap, we believe *the secret* to a strong body is a strong center. If your core muscles are tied to your vestibular system, it only makes sense that a healthy vestibular system is crucial to having a strong center; a strong center makes the whole X strong. The healthier our vestibular system is, the healthier and more resilient our bodies will become.

So, how do we train our vestibular system and develop a strong core? *We move!* We run, we jump, we spin, we roll, we flip, we rock. We move our heads! We do anything but sit in a chair for most of the day while we try to keep our heads still.

In fact, we believe there are certain "mid-line crossing" moves that can *"reset"* the body and stimulate the vestibular system with a proprioceptive flood of information. In other words, we believe we can press "reset" with certain movements to regain, and re-earn, the body we were meant to have.

Pressing "Reset"

*T*wo halves make a whole. Your brain has two hemi-spheres, the right hemisphere, or the gestalt side, and the left hemisphere, or the logic side. For your body to be efficient at anything, both hemispheres need to work together.[25] Performing midline crossing movements, also known as cross-lateral movements, seems to increase the communication between the two hemispheres.[26] Midline crossing movements can actually cause the brain to make new neural connections between the two hemispheres. This is what makes midline crossing movements crucial for learning and brain development. We believe it is also what makes them crucial for physical development. The more neural connections between the two hemispheres, the better the hemispheres work together and communicate with the body (i.e. the better you move). The more you tie your X together.

Midline crossing movements are movements like crawling, running, skipping, and walking. In these movements, the opposite arm moves with the opposite leg in a coordinated motion, *usually* to get you from one point to another point. The first midline crossing movement we would like to introduce to you is known as the *cross-crawl.* It is a phenomenal tool for making the brain and body more efficient.

Cross-crawls are a midline crossing movement where you take the opposite hand, or elbow, and touch it to the opposite knee.[27] They can be done sitting, standing, or lying down. The magic behind cross crawls is that they activate large areas of both hemispheres of the brain simultaneously.[28] And, when done on a regular, consistent basis, they actually improve the neural connections between the hemispheres, allowing for faster communication between the hemispheres and better communication between the brain and the body.[29] Cross crawls have even been instrumental in successfully helping patients recover from strokes and helping children overcome ADD and ADHD.[30]

Cross-crawling encourages better neural connections and even new nerve cell growth in the brain! And, you don't have to have a learning disability or a stroke to perform them. Anyone can improve their brain function and their body with cross-crawls because the healthier the brain becomes, the healthier the body becomes. This simple movement highlights the statement, movement *is* life.

Crawling is another midline crossing movement that **most** of us should have done as a child. Research has shown that those who skip crawling are more likely to have learning disorders.[31] They are more likely to have movement and coordination issues as well because crawling sets the foundation for the gait pattern. The beautiful thing about crawling is that you don't have to be a baby to do it. Anyone can learn how to crawl.

Though similar to cross-crawls, crawling offers other benefits as well. Through mechanoreceptors, nerve endings, in the hands and feet, crawling stimulates reflexive core musculature activation, which gets the shoulders and pelvis working together.[32]

Crawling can also improve your binocular vision, your hand-eye coordination, and even your binaural hearing (your perception of sound from two ears).[33] In *The Well Balanced Child,* Sally Goddard Blythe points out that "Movement on all fours also helps to align the spine at the back of the neck with the sacral region in preparation for proper alignment in the upright posture."[34] Crawling helps lay the foundation, on multiple levels, of who we become. In our discussions about becoming bulletproof and regaining our original strength, my friend, Mike McNiff, said that "We are simply trying to outsmart what we were designed to do." What a true statement! How many parents like to brag about how fast their kids learn to walk? How many parents try to hasten the process by putting their kids in walkers or other contraptions to encourage walking? We were meant to crawl, and with good reason. In today's world, crawling should probably be done by everyone, everyday, young and old alike. It can be a great tool for building a resilient, capable body.

I know what you're thinking: *But babies learn to crawl so they can walk. We were made and designed to walk on two feet. Babies progress to walking! We are not supposed to keep crawling around as adults!*

<u>You're absolutely right!</u> **But**, we're not supposed to sit around all day either. And yet, that is what most of us do. Yes, walking and running are both a mid-line crossing movement that require coordination and they should incorporate both hemispheres of our brains. But, you know what? **You can fake walking and running.** You can walk and run without using your shoulders and arms properly. You can even do it without using them at all. **<u>You cannot fake crawling</u>.** It is deliberate.

Your shoulders and hips have to work together. With crawling, they are both working together under load. Crawling sets things right, the way they were meant to be. It is the foundation, the template, for our gait pattern. Crawling is the ultimate "reset" pattern. It helps keep the center of our X, our center, functioning properly.

As great as crawling is, we have found that some clients just cannot crawl well; they have zero coordination. We have also had other clients that just didn't seem to get as big of a bang for their buck from crawling. Turns out, crawling is not the first thing we start doing when we start learning how to move. We rock before we crawl. We roll before we rock. And, we raise our heads before we roll. Some people, maybe all people, should spend some time rocking and rolling! Others should spend some time learning how to raise and move their heads and stimulating their vestibular system.

Gray Cook has a DVD called *Secrets of the Primitive Patterns*. In discussing movement issues, he states that you can fix a lot of issues by correcting primitive patterns.[35]

Rolling is a primitive pattern. It is how most of us first learn to traverse the floor as babies. Rolling stimulates the vestibular system in a big way. (Remember, the vestibular system is tied to the core muscles.) Rolling also helps us develop rotary trunk stability - the ability for our trunk to remain stable under asymmetrical and contralateral loads - a critical component for spine health. It prepares us for gait; crawling, walking, and running. We have witnessed rolling address several movement issues in clients. (These movement issues were revealed by using Gray Cook's Functional Movement Screen - The FMS). We have also witnessed dramatic improvements in strength, movement efficiency, stability, endurance and resiliency thanks to teaching clients how to roll.

Rocking, though not a midline crossing movement, is another primitive pattern that is perhaps one of the biggest resets. Rocking, or Quadruped Rocking, prepares the body for crawling. Not only that, it seems to really help with pelvic and scapular stabilization, and it may help align the spine.[36] Basically, rocking is a great way to start tying the core / body together. Rocking is done by getting on your hands and knees, keeping a long spine (head and chest up!) and rocking your butt back towards your calves. As we mentioned earlier, rocking is a tremendous reset. This drill can unlock a world of movement function for people. Rocking is also good for opening up the hips and re- engaging the deep and abdominal muscles - like the pelvic floor and *transverse abdominus* - muscles that have been identified as dysfunctional in lower back pain populations and mothers. It also helps develop, or redevelop good posture, a point we'll address later when we look at rocking more closely.

Rolling, rocking, crawling, and cross crawling are all great tools for pressing the "reset button" for the body. Using the Functional Movement Screen (FMS)[37] as an assessment tool for our clients, we have found that these midline crossing movements have been great for restoring movement patterns, addressing asymmetries and correcting other movement issues and dysfunctions. They have even helped some of our clients with some instances of pain. If you want to get your body functioning like it was meant to and you want to become fully connected and integrated, in every sense, these movements work wonders.

Dan John, a famous strength coach and author, taught Tim a very valuable lesson:

If something is important, you should do it everyday.[38]

These four movements are important. **Do** them every day. It all adds up: They can truly help unlock your potential and put you on your way towards regaining your original strength.

Before we go any deeper on the resets, let's take a look at the one reset that was *intended* to be automatic for you: *Walking*.

The Automatic Reset

*A*s we briefly discussed in the previous chapter, we were made to walk - on two feet. Walking is the midline-crossing movement, the reset, that you were designed to do. Walking should be your everyday reset. Unfortunately, for most, that may not be the case:

One of the things that makes crawling so wonderful is that it does require us to use our shoulders and pelvis together in a coordinated fashion, it helps establish great posture, and it truly is the foundation of our gait pattern. Crawling prepares us to traverse the world on two feet. Crawling ties our core together. With this "tied-together core," we are supposed to get up and walk effortlessly and efficiently transferring force from the ground, up through our core, and into and out of our arms.

Let's be honest: How much walking do we really do? Two thousand years ago people were bulletproof. Okay, there were no bullets 2000 years ago, but people were a lot more *resilient* then than we are today. Back then, people walked almost everywhere they went. They didn't hop in a car

> **Resilient** - re-sil-ient (ri'zilyent) - *adjective*
>
> Able to withstand or recover quickly from difficult conditions.

or on a couch. These people were tough! Walking helped keep them resilient.

Think about it. People once built amazing structures like pyramids and coliseums. There were no machines: No bulldozers, no F-150s, no cars. There were people with strong backs and legs of steel. Their bodies were made out of iron. They moved, they worked, and they walked. If they needed a reset every now and then, they probably got it from all the walking around they did.

Today, most of us don't walk so much. And when we do, we are not necessarily walking the way we are designed to walk. We are not standing tall with good posture. We are not swinging our arms from our shoulders. Half the time most of us don't even swing our arms. Instead, we slouch, we look down at the ground, our smart phone, or we keep our hands in our pockets. We are not walking *deliberately* with purpose, the way we were made to walk.

Lions *are* lions. They are beautiful, strong, and graceful because they act like lions. What I mean by *walking with purpose* is that we should walk like the pinnacle creations that we are. We are kings and queens. We are the top of the food chain. We are **the** predators. We should not walk around as if we are the prey. Just as lions are lions, we should walk as kings and queens. We *are* conquerors.

Walking *is* **the reset** we were designed to do daily! We just don't do it so well. Today, because of our lifestyles, we are not well connected and tied together. Until we are, we may need to perform more intentional, foundational resets like crawling or cross-crawling. But in the meantime, start walking intentionally. Swing your arms from your shoulders. Allow your shoulders and hips to work together like they do when you crawl. Stand tall. Keep a long spine like you do when you are rocking. Keep the crown of your head pointing to the sky. (Don't worry, this will become virtually automatic once you start doing the rest of the resets. Hold on, we'll get to them in a minute. . .)

Seriously, make time in your day to start taking purposeful walks. Not only can this be a reseting, midline crossing exercise, it can be a mentally freeing and rejuvenating one as well. Walking can be like playing. Walking can set things right. Walking should be the automatic reset.

This may take time to sink in, but there is no way around it: in the end, ***we were made to walk!***

However, we do have to crawl before we walk. With that in mind, let's look at the resets!

We were made to walk. . ..

. . ..with contra-lateral limb movement!

How to Press "Reset"

I t is time to take a look at the resets. Most of these are the same resets found in *Becoming Bulletproof*. However, some have been added and some have been expanded upon to show alternatives and as well as some progressions. I think it is also wise to present them in a more "child-like" developmental fashion: From lying to standing, or crawl before walking approach. Keep in mind though, regardless of the order they are presented, resets do not necessarily need to be performed in any specific order. The order and the freedom of exploring the resets are individual specific.

Neck Nods - The Controversial Reset

At the time we're writing this book (2013) there is a trend in the fitness industry towards making the simple complicated - especially when it comes to the neck. In fact, some of the recommendations are based on the faulty interpretations of the body's function overall, including the design of the neck, it's relation to the rest of the body, and its amazing integration with the body's reflexes.

When you watch a child develop - not just watch one on a video or study pictures of one in books - but actually live with one 24/7, you'll notice one thing about a baby - he keeps his head up. His head position is determined by his eye position. Wherever his gaze is, his head follows. He looks up, his head follows and his neck moves into extension. He looks down, and his neck moves into flexion. Look left or right? His head rotates. This is normal and natural. This strengthens his neck muscles, his upper and lower back, and his abs, especially in the early months when he's practicing "tummy time," lying on his stomach and keeping his head up. For a baby, learning how to control his head is critical for his development of posture, balance, and coordination. If we combine those three words into one we would call it strength.

Because your ability to control your head, to have strength in your neck's extensors and [deep] flexors affects your posture, balance, and coordination, it affects your whole body.

When you lose full and reflexive control of your head and neck, you'll notice poor posture, a loss of balance (one of the first signs of aging), and decreased coordination in everything from your reflexes to the visual tracking necessary to catch a ball to a loss of mobility in the rest of your joints, like the thoracic spine, shoulders, hips, and ankles.

Neck nods are very simple to perform. Our basic neck nod starts on all fours - quadruped. (They can be performed in many other positions.) Simply look down and tuck your chin to your chest, keeping your arms straight then look up with your eyes and lift your head as high as you can, chin in the air. (Make sure to keep your tongue behind your teeth - its natural resting place - to protect your neck.) And repeat back and forth and back and forth and back and forth.

You'll find that neck nods can unlock a sticky t-spine, grease or pry open rusty hips, and even help unlock frozen ankles. Such is the power of using your head!

Incidentally posture improves and you no longer have to worry about using your cues. Posture, the posture you were designed to have when walking, just happens. Automatically. Like it's supposed to.

Somehow we've lost sight of this developmental process - the need and ability to control the head in any position and we have gone to what we call "artificial neutral" - or trying to keep the head and neck in its natural position during gait (walking) while performing other activities. We use terms like "neutral spine," and "long spine" and "pack the neck" to maintain the same head position we find while walking and transfer it into all other activities. This is not a good thing. We'll get into this concept in detail later. That's one of the points of neck nods: They help restore your reflexes so you don't have to worry about head and neck position. Your body does what comes naturally - what it's *supposed* to do without you having to think about it.

Neck Nods:

- Start on your hands and knees like your about to crawl (quadruped)
- Place your tongue against the back of your top teeth and on the roof of your mouth and keep it there the whole time
- Look down at the floor and tuck your chin to your chest
- Look up at the ceiling with your eyes first and try to get your face parallel with the ceiling (Not going to happen, but at least you have something to shoot for)
- Go back and forth between looking down and up
- Play around with diaphragmatic breathing while performing your nods - pausing and breathing in each position

Pictures of Neck Nods

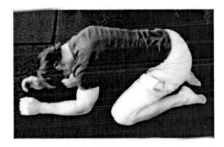
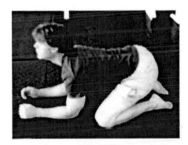

Neck Nods can be done on the forearms, the hands,
or even lying down.

Rolling

Rolling is simply the act of lying on the floor and transitioning from your belly to your back and from your back to your belly. There are more ways to roll than there are letters in the alphabet. But first, because it works wonders in restoring reflexive strength and movement patterns, we will look at rolling the way Gray Cook outlines in his book, *Movement*.

Segmental Rolling:[39]

- Back to Belly Rolling - Upper Body:
  - Lie on your back with your legs straight and your arms straight over head.
  - **Using your head**, neck and right arm, reach across your body as far as you can and roll to your belly. **Do not cheat and use your legs!**
  - Can you do this with equal movement and effort with both arms?

- Belly to Back Rolling - Upper Body:
  - Lie on your belly with your legs straight and your arms straight overhead.

- **Use your head**, neck and right arm to reach back across your body and roll to your back. **Do not cheat and use your legs!**
- Can you do this with equal movement and effort with both arms?

- Back to Belly Rolling - Lower Body:
  - Lie on your back with your legs straight and your arms straight over head.
  - Using your right leg, reach across your body and roll to your belly. **Do not cheat and use your arms!**
  - Can you do this with equal movement and effort with both legs?

- Belly to Back Rolling - Lower Body:
  - Lie on your belly with your legs straight and your arms straight over head.
  - Use your right leg to reach back across your body and roll to your back. **Do not cheat and use your arms!**
  - Can you do this with equal movement and effort with both legs?

Pictures of the Segmental Roll

Back to Belly and Belly to Back Upper Body Rolls

Back to Belly Lower Body Roll

Belly to Back Lower Body Roll

Even though babies don't roll this way, segmental rolling is a great place to start when it comes to rolling. We like to start with this method because it can both expose movement issues and unlock movement issues at the same time. We have witnessed rolling "fix", or clean up an entire Functional Movement Screen Score[40] in several of our clients. This makes sense because rolling is one of the first ways we start to learn and "earn" our movements and movement patterns as infants. It can also be a great way to re-learn and re-earn them again.

Tim likes to have his clients roll 3 times from each limb, in both directions. If a client has a hard time rolling, we know what we need to work on. He typically gives rolling as "homework." He likes for his clients to be able to fluidly roll from one side to the other with all their limbs with the same ease.

Once segmental rolling can be performed with ease, other forms of rolling can be introduced. The following rolls are more advanced rolls. These are just examples of different ways to roll. They need not be performed if pressing the reset button on the body is all that is desired. However, they may make the reset button even stronger. These rolling variations also provide a fun, playful way to explore the bodies movement capabilities while at the same time, they sharpen and improve the bodies ability to move.

The Hard Roll:[41]

- Lie on your back with your right arm held straight overhead and your left leg held straight.
- If you have the mobility, touch and then press your left elbow to your right knee.
- Using your head, roll toward your right side.
- Once you have rolled to your right side, use your head again and roll back to your back (the starting position).
  - **Do not let your elbow and knee separate during the roll!** This is the Hard Roll!
  - Can you do this equally with right elbow against your left knee?

The hard roll earns its name for one reason: It is well, "hard" to do for most people. However, when the hard roll becomes easy, you can bet that your X is pretty well tied together! This roll can be great to play with, or you can simply use it as a gauge to see how well connected you are. As you can see from the pictures, the hard roll requires both strength and mobility.

Pictures of Hard Roll

In the beginning, initiate the roll using your head and neck.

When the hard roll becomes the "easy roll," you will be able to perform it without using your head at all!

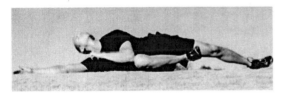

Don't let your elbow and knee separate!!!

The Neck Roll:

- While resting on your forearms and belly, use only your head and neck and roll over to your back with your legs straight and your arms resting over your chest.
- While lying on your back, use only your head and neck and roll to your belly.
  - You can "land" propped up on your forearms.
- Practice rolling in both directions.
- These can feel very good!

Pictures of Neck Rolls

Belly to Back Neck Roll

Back to Belly Neck Roll

Note:

This is just **one** way to perform a neck roll. Babies actually employ a different type of neck roll that we LOVE to do. However, because of the nature in which that particular neck roll is performed, we only like to demonstrate and teach it in public at our workshops.

The Elevated Roll:

- Assume the pushup position on your hands and feet.
- Use your right leg to reach back across your body and roll until your right foot rest on the ground.
- As you reach and roll with your right leg, your right hand will leave the ground.
- When your right foot makes contact with the ground, your right arm should end up pointing up at the sky.
- Push both feet into the ground and reach for the sky with your pelvis.
- When you are ready to return, REACH across your body with your right arm and pull your lower body back over to the starting pushup position.
- Can you do this with equal movement and effort with both legs and arms?

Pictures of the Elevated Roll

Just reverse the motion, leading with the arm, to return to the pushup position.

This roll feels fantastic! It can make a great "movement snack" to throw into the day every now and then.

Rocking

After rolling, let's look at rocking. *Rock and Roll!* Get it?

Rocking seems to be a high payoff "reset" for a lot of people. We have found that rocking really seems to help improve posture, reflexive stability, and mobility. Our good friend and famous author, Dan John, even credits rocking to regaining his strength and rehabbing his hip after having undergone hip surgery. Today Dan is competing in the Highland Games and is enjoying Olympic Lifting, his passion. Rocking helped Dan rebuild his body and regain his original strength!

The way we like to teach people how to rock is to have them get down on their hands and knees, keep a BIG chest, keep the crown of their head pointed to the sky (head held up) and rock their butt back towards their calves.

Rocking is literally simply rocking back and forth. In the beginning, try it nice and slow. As you get comfortable with it, you can play with the speed in which you rock. As your hips loosen up, you can also play with the width in which you place your knees by moving them closer together or farther apart. You can also rock using different foot positions. There really is not "one way" to rock. Playing with the different rocking positions can be very relaxing and therapeutic.

As relaxing and gentle as it is, rocking really ties the body together. In fact, you can see for yourself how this works. If you want to see how your muscles are wired to your neck, do some head nods while you are sitting back towards your calves. You will feel your whole back musculature "turn on." If you try to look over your shoulders to see your own butt, you will even feel the muscles around your scapula sink the scapula down towards your butt. Head position facilitates muscle actions / contractions. Play with it a little and you will see what we mean.

Rocking back and forth also really seems to engage the pelvic floor. That is to say that rocking seems to cause the pelvic floor muscles to fire reflexively. Many people notice this as they push their butt back towards their calves. This is a huge benefit as real strength originates from the center of our X. Original strength happens between a properly functioning diaphragm and a properly functioning pelvic floor. If the dia-phragm is working well because we are breathing properly, and the pelvic floor is functioning well reflexively, then we have a recipe for a very strong body. So, while rocking is a great reset, practicing diaphragmatic breathing while rocking, can be a tremendous reset!

Not only that, we've found that rocking seems to engage the abs from the inside out, especially when your weight is forward in your hands. What we mean is that not only can you feel your deep abdominal muscles working, but you can also feel your "six pack" working when you really start getting into rocking.

Rocking is a fantastic drill. It helps improve reflexive stability throughout entire body. It also improves proprioception, posture, and hip mobility. The benefits of rocking can be fairly immediate. It is an effective drill to perform between sets of squats, deadlifts, or kettlebell swings as it really seems to "clean up" movement.

How to Perform Rocking:

- Start on your hands and knees as if you are about to crawl.
- In the beginning, place the tops of your feet on the ground (plantar flex your feet)
- Keep a tall chest, like Billy Bodybuilder on the beach.
- Hold your head up so that you can see the horizon.
- Push your butt back towards your feet.
    - Play with head nods while holding the bottom position of the rock.
    - Play with diaphragmatic breathing while holding the bottom position of the rock.
- Move in and out, back and forth, slowly - at first.
    - Play with different speeds as you get used to the motion.

<u>Pictures of Rocking</u>

Starting position   *Ending position*

for rocking   *for rocking*

Rocking on Hands and Feet

- Start on your hands and feet as if you are about to Spider-man crawl.
- Keep a tall chest, like Billy Bodybuilder on the beach.
- Hold your head up so that you can see the horizon.
- Push your butt back towards your feet.
    - Make sure you keep a BIG chest!!!
    - Play with head nods while holding the bottom position of the rock.
    - Play with diaphragmatic breathing while holding the bottom position of the rock.
- Move in and out, back and forth, slowly - at first.
    - Play with different speeds as you get used to the motion.

Pictures of Rocking on Hands and Feet

Starting position   *Ending position*

Crawling

Crawling is probably Tim's favorite reset because it seems to yield fantastic results for a lot of people. This is probably because crawling is much more than just a reset. It is also gentle strength training. When a baby crawls, or an adult for that matter, they are earning and developing their strength by literally tying their bodies, their X, together. This happens because every time the hands or feet touch the ground, the proprioceptors (nerves) in the hands and feet stimulate reflexive contractions throughout the body's musculature. In other words, crawling reflexively stimulates the muscles throughout your body and ties them all together, especially the muscles in your center. This creates a reflexively strong body and prepares the body to transfer force! Yes, believe it or not, crawling like a baby can make your body powerful!

Crawling simply fills in "the gaps" in your body. It lays a strong foundation of strength and mobility from which you can build a resilient, healthy, strong and powerful body. Beyond the gentle, reflexive strength building nature of crawling, crawling also forces the hips and shoulders to work together. Not only is this important because it helps us to become powerful, it also sets the foundation for our gait patterns: Walking, skipping, running, and climbing. Crawling is the template for how we walk and run. ***Remember, if you are not crawling well,*** ***you are probably not walking and running well either!***

We know what you're thinking: "Crawling? This is so simple, even a baby can do it." And, you're absolutely right. A baby can do it, through practice and effort. But you, however, may not be able to do it quite so well. It turns out that a lifetime of not crawling combined with tons of sitting and no running can make crawling quite frustrating for adults. There are some of you reading this right now who cannot crawl well. Others of you may find that you can crawl forward well, but you can't crawl backwards to save your life! Crawling is simple, but it is not necessarily easy - in the beginning.

Having said that, there are different ways to crawl and there is benefit in spending time in exploring each different type of crawl. Some of you will be strong enough to Spider- man crawl from the start, yet you will lack the coordination. If this is you, you need to spend time mastering the baby crawl. Others of you may have knee issues, or other physical issues that make baby crawling uncomfortable at best. If this is you, you may need to spend time commando crawling.

When it comes to crawling, use patience and GOOD judge-ment. Just because you think one type of crawl may look "cooler," or "sexier" than another, you need to spend time crawling **where you need to.** We say this because many people want to jump right to the Spider-man crawl. And to be honest, that is Tim's favorite crawl (He likes to pretend that he is Spider-man). The Spider-man crawl will build the body of your dreams. However, this may not be where you need to start out at.

Spider-man crawling presents more of a challenge to some people as it can be harder to learn and it takes more strength to perform. It also places more load on the shoulder girdle than most people probably need if they are **only** trying to press reset. Again, Spider-man crawling is fantastic, ***but*** it should be reserved as a higher order reset and not attempted until it poses no stress or frustration on the part of the crawler. If it makes sense that we have to crawl before we walk, it should also make sense that we may need to baby crawl before we Spider-man crawl. Or, we may need to even start out with commando crawling before we baby crawl. Again, use good judgement and be honest with yourself.

If you are in doubt as to whether or not you have good judgement, do not fret! Just start out with the easiest way to crawl and don't move on until you are good with it. Also, remember this: <u>If you are only trying to press reset, the baby crawl is all</u>

<u>you need.</u> You don't need to perform the harder crawls unless you just want to.

Now, let's learn how to crawl!

Crawling:
- Crawling can be done on the hands and knees, like a baby, on your forearms and legs - commando style, or on the hands and feet, like Spider-man.
  - Remember, Spider-man crawling is a higher order reset and it should be reserved until you are strong enough to perform them without stress or frustration.
- When crawling, keep your head held up - crown of your head to the sky, and keep your chest up like you are proud.
- Move your opposite limbs together.
  - Your opposite arm should move with your opposite leg - contra-lateral limb movement.
  - If this is not natural to you, rest, relax, focus, and try again. It will come!

Pictures of Crawling

Commando Crawling, or Army Crawling.

Baby Crawling

Pictures of Crawling Continued

Leopard Crawling

Spider-man Crawling

Spider-man Crawling

Okay, we know we've already touched on this, but we just can't say enough about Spider-man crawling. We want to talk about its benefits a little more as we feel they can easily be missed due to the simplicity of this wonderful movement.

Spider-man crawling can be a tremendous reset for the body, especially when the body is ready and strong enough to engage in it. That is why it was presented in this section. However, Spider-man crawling can also be a tremendous strength builder. It is probably one of the best ways to really tie the body together - from a strength standpoint as well as a neurological standpoint. And this may be why we love Spider-man crawling so much: You can actually *reset* your body and build a tremendously strong body at the same time.

Spider-man crawling will develop *real* abs of steel. To say it another way, it builds a rock-solid center and ties the X, the body, together. To review again, Spider-man crawling is done on the hands and feet with the butt held in a low position. The butt is down low, and the head is up to see where you are going. Just holding your body in this position takes strength. Getting used to being in this position builds strength. Reflexively, every time your hands and feet - especially if you are barefoot - touch the ground, you reinforce strength and dynamic stability by putting pressure on the proprioceptors (nerves) in your palms and feet.

You can see this for yourself. Watch someone Spider-man crawl. You will notice that their triceps and lats contract as soon as their hands hit the ground. This is also happening in the muscles that you cannot see like the muscles of the rotator cuff and the muscles of the inner and outer obliques. Spider-man crawling literally ties the core, the entire body, together and prepares it to transfer force.

As I said, with the Spider-man crawl, you can press reset and build strength at the same time. Sure, you can just use the Spider-man crawl as a reset and include it in your warm-up, cool-down, or daily movement program, but you can also use it as a stand- alone strength training session. If you don't believe me, just try Spider-man crawling for 5 straight minutes. If you achieve one minute off the bat, I'll be really impressed! If you try this, you will notice that Spider-man crawling takes strength, stamina, a good heart and a good set of lungs. The good news is that Spider-man crawling also builds these things. It gives improves and gives vitality to the entire body.

Another benefit of Spider-man crawling is that it is pretty much like "horizontal" climbing. Climbing is another way to build a fully capable, strong body, as it also ties the body together. Sadly though, most of us don't climb, nor do we have access to a place where we can climb. This is what makes Spider-man crawling so great: you can do it anywhere, and if you fall, you're already on the ground! Not only that, but Spider-man crawling is easy to progress. You can do it backwards, sideways, slow, or fast. You can crawl for time and distance. You can even add resistance and drag things while you crawl if you want to. The sky is the limit.

Have we said enough about Spider-man crawling? We really like it, can you tell? You really can use it as a tool to build the body of your dreams. BUT REMEMBER, you probably shouldn't dive into it until your body is ready for it. If you are not coordinated enough, or strong enough, be patient and start with commando or baby crawling first.

And if you don't like Spider-man crawling as much as we do, that is okay. The important thing is to crawl often. Crawl anyway you like - every day. Crawling helps builds a better brain, a more efficient nervous system, and a stronger body capable of moving more efficiently. Crawling is a powerful reset and it plays a pivotal role in regaining your original strength.

It doesn't matter how silly you feel, or how silly other people think you look. Just get down and crawl.

The Leopard Crawl - A Transitional Reset

Truth be told, most people just can't handle the Spider-man crawl, as much as they want to think they can. And even if they can, they won't be able to do it nearly as effortlessly as Tim makes it look. Their hips go all wobbly and most of their movement comes from rotating at their lumbar spine. Not good. For those who have no problem Baby crawling, they still can't perform the Spider-man crawl, they need something in between. Especially if you've ever had a lower back injury or lower back pain.

That's because the Spider-man crawl takes a very high degree of core muscle coordination that is only "bought" through high levels of reflexive stability, something most people who sit all day don't have.

Enter the Leopard crawl.

We call it the Leopard crawl because it reminds us of one of our favorite big cats - the leopard.

It's similar to a Bear crawl, only the hips are held down below the head, just like the Spiderman crawl, but instead of having the knees go to the outside of the elbows, they stay inside. This still works the daylights out of the legs, lungs, hips, and core, but does requires less reflexive stability, while building it at the same time.

Because of his hip and lower back injuries, Geoff literally spent two years on the Leopard crawl before he could successfully transition to the Spider-man crawl.

And don't worry, it's equally as challenging as the Spider-man crawl - and just as beneficial. And just like the Spider-man crawl, all the different variations apply - backward, sideways, slow or fast; for time or distance. Your creativity is your only constraint.

Cross-Crawl and other Mid-line Crossing Movements

Cross-crawls are nothing new. You've probably even done them before in gym class. Athletes have been using them off and on for years as part of a warm-up routine. Chiropractors like Dr. Leroy Perry, the first chiropractor ever to serve as an Olympic Team Doctor, have always known that they benefit the body. But for the most part, cross-crawls have really only been recognized for how they benefit the brain, not so much for how they benefit the body physically. For years, cross-crawls have been used to treat learning disabilities in children as well as help stroke patients regain their normal function. It is quite amazing how such a simple move can cause growth and development in the brain. It is also quite amazing how the brain is capable of growth and development at any age! Remember this: If you improve the brain, you improve the body. And if you improve the body, you improve the brain.

A cross-crawl is done by walking in place while touching your opposite elbow to your opposite knee. In doing so, you are crossing mid-line of the body and activating both hemispheres of your brain with the coordinated movement. Cross-crawls are really just the crawling pattern done while standing.

There are many different ways to perform the cross crawl. This is great, because we all have many different bodies and abilities. You can choose the cross crawl that is right for you based on your ability to perform it. This is one of the factors that makes cross crawls so effective. Anyone can do them, and they are easy to progress.

Cross-crawls can be performed in almost any position that you can put your body into. Cross-crawls can be performed in a chair, on the floor while lying on your back, while standing, walking, or even while skipping. If you cannot touch your opposite elbow to your opposite knee, you simply touch your opposite hand or forearm to your opposite knee or thigh. If you do not have the balance to perform the cross-crawl while standing, try it lying down on your back and do cross-crawl sit-ups. No matter what your abilities or physical limitations, you should be able to find a way to perform a cross-crawl.

Cross-crawls can easily be progressed to more challenging versions. For instance, if you have no trouble touching your elbow to your knee while standing, try doing them while you keep your fingertips behind your ears. If keeping your fingertips behind your ears is easy, try doing that with your eyes closed or with your eyes looking in the opposite direction of where you are rotating towards. Try cross-crawling marching forward, try cross-crawling while marching backwards, try them super slow, try them while skipping or even while skipping *and* spinning around in circles. You can even try them while eating green eggs and ham! Just kidding! Anyway, the more you can progress with your cross-crawls, the more coordination you are developing. However, you don't have to get fancy with your cross-crawls if you don't want to, they will still work. But, if you want to get as much out of them as you can, have fun and progress them. Just make sure you do them!

Cross-Crawls

- Cross-crawls can be done sitting, lying, standing, or while walking or skipping.
- Simply touch your opposite elbow to your opposite knee.
  - If your mobility does not allow for you to touch opposite elbow to knee, you can touch opposite hand or forearm to opposite knee or thigh.
  - If your mobility does allow, you can also try performing them with your finger tips behind your ears.
- Perform them slow unless you are skipping.

Pictures of Cross-Crawls:

Various ways of per-

forming cross-crawls

Marching and Skipping

Marching and skipping are other mid-line crossing, contra-lateral, movements like cross- crawls. The difference with marching and skipping is that there is no touching of the opposite limbs. Marching and skipping, are however, fantastic resets as they require deliberate movement and coordination between the opposite limbs. When done properly, they gets the hips and shoulders working together much in the same way that crawling does. You could even say that marching and skipping are like a "standing crawl."

Skipping, as well as marching, is also a great movement preparation for sprinting - another reset, a beautiful power producing reset! Skipping introduces the body to gentle bounding and rebounding. This can be a great preparatory tool should you ever decide to sprint or engage in life - outside, in the real world.

How to March:
Marching can be done in a variety of ways, but I prefer the following method:

- Hold your elbows at 90 degrees.
- Drive your arms from your shoulders and ensure that they are moving from front to back.

- Really focus on driving the arms back to get good extension.
  - Your back hand should be able to tap your "back pocket."
- The opposite arm should drive forward as the opposite knee drives upward.
- Plant and push off of the balls of your feet when marching.
- The rise of the knees should match the height and drive of the arm.
- The arms and legs should move crisply.

How to Skip:

Skipping can also be done in a variety of ways, but I still prefer the following method:

- Hold your elbows at 90 degrees.
- Drive your arms from your shoulders and ensure that they are moving from front to back.
- Really focus on driving the arms back to get good extension.
  - Your back hand should be able to tap your "back pocket."
- The opposite arm should drive forward as the opposite knee drives upward, lifting your body off the ground.
- Plant and push off of the balls of your feet when skipping.
- Land and absorb impact on the ground with the balls of the feet as well.
- The rise of the knees should match the height and drive of the arm.
- The arms and legs should move crisply.

Pictures of Marching:

Pictures of Skipping:

Look above and just imagine that I am floating in the air and my feet are off the ground! They "look" pretty similar.

Sprinting

As I just alluded to, sprinting can also be reset, especially when the body is tied together the way it should be. After all, sprinting is the ultimate expression of our gait pattern. Sprinting embodies and expresses everything our bodies were designed to be: Powerful, graceful, beautiful, and strong. There is nothing more beautiful than a sprinting body in motion.

<u>Sprinting should be a reset!</u>

But, it is probably not a reset for you - *just yet.*

But it can be!

Like crawling, sprinting nourishes the brain and encourages communication between our brain's hemispheres. It even helps build reflexive strength, at a higher level of force. Sprinting is our ultimate tool for becoming resilient as it prepares our bodies to explode: To create, absorb and transfer high forces at high speeds. In other words, sprinting prepares us for life and all the physical demands life throws at us.

Believe it or not, *you were made to sprint!*

When you learned to crawl and walk as a child, you were laying the foundation for coordination, strength and power. You were preparing your body to create and transfer powerful forces. You were preparing your body to sprint.

It is true. Somewhere inside of you, there is a sprinter. However, you may not be ready to wake that sprinter up just yet. Because of its demands, the powerful nature of sprinting and the forces that it generates, you want to make sure your body is prepared to sprint should you ever decide to sprint. You need a solid foundation to handle the beautiful power that sprinting generates. How do you do this? The same way you did as a child. You spend some time performing the previous resets and recreate a solid foundation, the solid foundation, that you once had. Once you have tied your body back together, you will be ready to sprint. And then, once you are tied back together, sprinting can be a wonderful reset for you as well.

Be patient! When you are ready, when you have pressed reset enough times and have tied your X together, "play" with sprinting. "Play" here means to *explore*. Explore what it is like to sprint. In the beginning, if you have never sprinted much, start out with *gentle* **skipping**. You can use skipping as a way to ease your way into the idea of sprinting. As your confidence increases, move into more forceful skipping, where you generate more explosive power. Then later, when you are ready, you can engage in sprinting at half speed and work your way up to three-quarter speed. When half speed and three-quarter speed starts to feel really good, you may be ready for full speed! <u>But again, be patient and work your way up to this over time</u>. It may take days, weeks, or months before you are ready. That's okay. Enjoy the process.

Sprinting - perhaps the ultimate expression of our design: power, efficiency, and beauty.

Before you dismiss whether or not sprinting is for you, keep this in your mind: *You were made to sprint.* If you are capable of sprinting, you should probably sprint. If you are not yet capable of sprinting, you need to build a solid movement foundation (spend some time pressing reset) and work to become able to sprint. You will be glad you did. It is after all, a higher-order reset. It is good for the brain and good for the body. Besides, there is nothing more exhilarating than feeling like you can fly as you float across the ground. You were meant to move this way - with beautiful power. You were meant to sprint. Don't deny yourself!

Reset Your Feet!

*R*emember, everything about your body is completely integrated. When we purposefully set out to press reset, we should try to take advantage of our integrated design. We should give our brain and body as much information as possible.

If everything about your body is integrated, it would make sense that regaining our original strength requires a multi-faceted approach. Having said that, your feet play no small part when it comes to building a resilient body. Believe it or not, *we are born without shoes.* Yes, it is true. When you came into the world, your feet were bare. They were perfectly made to grasp the ground and give you a platform on which to stand. Feet, much like the hands, are full of nerve endings that send proprioceptive information to your brain. In other words, the nerves in your feet help paint a picture in your brain of where your body is and what it is doing.

When you learned to crawl, or traverse the floor, your feet sent all kinds of information to your brain about what your body was doing. Your feet sent information to your leg muscles and your core muscles as well and they helped establish some of your movement patterns. Remember, everything about you is tied together. Nothing is isolated. Your feet have sensory nerves and proprioceptors to help complete the "body map" in your brain.

Remember the analogy of the 3D map of your body inside your brain? The more clear the map is, the better you move. If the map is fuzzy, you may not move so well. If you are getting good information from all your sensory nerves in your skin, joints and muscles, your movement map will be clearer. If you are not getting good information from your sensory nerves, your movement map will get fuzzy.

Shoes can make your movement map fuzzy because they prevent your feet from feeling the world. Shoes do not allow your feet to feel the ground. Shoes do not allow your feet to move as they were designed to move. Shoes do not allow your foot muscles to work the way they were designed. There are nerves in our skin, muscles and joints that all help paint the picture of our movement map. A shoe effectively distorts all of these!

Your foot is amazing! It's made to bear weight - to support your entire body - and move. Essentially, it's your natural shock absorber. There are 26 bones, 33 joints, and more than 100 muscles, tendons, and ligaments in just one of your feet. A foot obviously has skin to protect us, as well as give our brain feedback for the environment we are in. Shoes more often than not compress the feet, prohibiting the muscles form functioning properly and the joints from moving through their full ranges of motion. This distorts the proprioceptive information being received by the brain. It also weakens the muscles in the foot. (Use it or lose it!) This can cause us to become flat-footed because we lose our arches, those wonderfully strong structures that are made to withstand huge amounts of compressive force.[42] Shoes also distort the sensory information being given by the skin.

If our goal is to become as resilient as possible, it may be a good idea to spend some time barefooted, especially when you train. Remember, everything about you is connected. All of our proprioceptive information gets routed through our vestibular system first, *and* our vestibular system is connected to our core musculature. It would only be a small leap of faith to think that your feet are connected to your core as well. The truth is they are! Pavel Tsatsouline points out, ". . .Another power boosting reflex is called the positive support reaction.

This reflex causes the leg musculature to contract in response to the pressure on the sole of the foot."[43] Pavel also goes on to mention the *extensor reflex* which causes the leg muscles to fire in a precise pattern depending on how the foot hits the ground.[44] The leg muscles are indeed part of the core, and they certainly would affect how forces travel from the ground through the core. You want your leg muscles prepared for the forces you are about to absorb and produce from the ground. In other words, *your feet are important!* They prepare the body for power, stability and strength. Shoes only distort, alter and slow information from the feet to the brain.

Again, going barefoot may be the way to go if you're trying to become bulletproof. I'm not saying you can never wear shoes, but I would suggest when you train, or play, you allow your feet to feel the ground. If the idea of being barefoot gives you the willies, you can always try barefoot shoes, or minimalist shoes. They will allow your foot to perform as it was designed. There are several new minimalist shoe options available now that the barefoot movement is catching on.

If you haven't spent anytime being barefoot since you were a toddler and you decide to give being barefoot a try, use common sense. *Ease your way into it.* Remember, *becoming bulletproof is a journey*, not a one time event. Your body and your feet will be grateful if you make this transition gradually. It is no different than beginning an exercise program, you ease your way into it to become successful.

From Tim:

I would like to add that crawling around on your hands and feet while you are barefooted is a great way to ease your feet into barefoot training. When you are crawling on your hands and feet, like Spider-man, you have considerably reduced the load on your feet. In other words, your feet get to "strength train" with only a fraction of your weight. Yet another benefit to crawling!

The Big 5

$\mathcal{Y}$ou might be thinking that there are a lot of resets. *How do you know which ones to do?* We won't lie, we are all individuals, you may need a reset that we don't or vise versa. However, we have found that most people seem to excel with the "Big 5." The Big 5 are neck nods, rolling, rocking, crawling and cross-crawling. These resets seem to offer the biggest bang for most people's buck when it comes to pressing reset. In truth, they are probably all you need to do when you are setting out to regain your original strength. In our own training, we use the Big 5 every day and we only "play" with the others every once in a while.

So, if you are feeling overwhelmed by the number of resets, relax, keep it simple and just stick with neck nods, rolling, rocking, crawling and cross-crawling - just start with the Big 5. As you get further along, you can always "play" with the other resets by adding them into your day here and there. You may find that you really enjoy exploring and experimenting with the different ways to press reset.

Now, that we have covered how to do the resets, let's look at how to incorporate them into your daily lifestyle.

It is ridiculously simple! So simple, you will be amazed and maybe even bewildered. . .

Pressing Reset Every Day

*W*hen it comes to regaining our original strength, numbers and repetitions add up. This is especially true when it comes to the brain and the body. Remember, the body and brain follow the "use it or lose it" principle, but they also follow the "use it and keep it" - *the engrave it* - principle. Everything about your brain and your body are the result of simple addition and subtraction.

If you make a movement, you create a neural pathway for that movement.[45] If you keep making that movement, you engrave that neural pathway in your brain. This is how habits are created. Through repetition, your body will also eventually adapt to that movement through the SAID principle (Specific Adaptation to Imposed Demand - it states that the body will adapt to the stresses that are placed on it).[46]

Conversely, when you don't make a movement, perhaps a movement that you used to make, your body eventually starts pruning those neural connections that were associated with that specific movement. This is called neural pruning.[47] When you are a teenager, neural pruning gets rid of all the unused neural connections in your brain; it's kind of like "spring cleaning" for the brain. As an adult, your neural connections may not be totally cleaned out and removed, but they do get weaker and less efficient. Hence the "use it or lose it" notion.

Your body is hungry for movement because movement is what provides your brain with the information of self awareness, self image, and your sense of self in space. Movement nourishes the brain. Not moving, like sitting for hours, weakens the neural connections of the movement vocabulary inside your brain. Essentially, not moving starves the brain.

Not moving starves the body as well. Not only does it weaken the neural connections between your brain and your body, it weakens the tissues in your body because you are no longer stimulating your proprioceptors or using your muscles, tendons, ligaments, and fascia as they were designed. The body adapts; the neural connections in your brain, the foundations of your movement vocabulary, get weaker and less efficient while your body adapts to the non-moving postures that you are getting very good at. The body and the brain are very good at adapting to the things we do, or don't do, because we are creations of efficiency.

In our world, it is difficult to overcome all of the *not moving* that we do. So, we must be deliberate in making movement a priority. Not only that, it makes sense that we should prioritize the movements we make and engage in the movements that would give us the biggest "neural bang for our buck", A.K.A. the Resets; specifically rolling, neck nods, rocking, crawling, and cross-crawls!

Remember, the Resets can actually create new neural connections in the brain and they also improve communication between the brain's hemispheres as well as communication between the brain and the body. For the most part, the resets are primitive patterns, or foundational patterns, that our movement vocabulary is built off. If we are good at performing the Resets, it would make sense that our movement vocabulary will be much broader than if we did not own our foundational patterns. In other words, owning our foundational patterns enables us to move in all the wonderful ways we were created to move.

This is where the Daily Reset comes into play. We can take advantage of the efficiency in which our brain and body operate. The brain is plastic. It is always changing. Every thought, every move you make, alters the structure of your brain in some way by creating a new neural connection.[48]

By performing the Resets every day, we can make those "Reset Movement" connections very efficient by engraving them, by strengthening them, through repetition. What does this mean? If cross-crawls make both brain hemispheres communicate with each other more effectively *and* they lay down new neural connections between the hemispheres, then performing them every single day solidifies those connections and the brain will become very efficient at cross-hemisphere communication. In other words, your brain will become more efficient, and you may actually become smarter![49] Also, performing the resets day after day, improves the neural connections between your body and your brain as well. Daily you are stimulating your proprioceptors, your vestibular system and your tissues. You are reinforcing your foundational patterns *and* improving your movement vocabulary through neural efficiency.

Huh? Daily Resets can improve **you** and all that you do. They can help you become bulletproof, or office proof, or age proof, or whatever else it is you aspire to do, to become, or overcome.

If you are not training, or playing with movement every day, you should at least engage in performing a Daily Reset. On the days you are out moving and living, you can perform a preparatory movement reset, also known as a warm-up! The goal should be to do *something* every single day. **_Consistency is the magic pill you need to swallow_**!

You can do this. It is ridiculously easy and simple. Take three minutes out of your day and "Press Reset" every day!

The Daily Reset:

1. Roll

- Perform segmental rolls from side to side, and from limb to limb. Perform 3 complete rolls from each limb.
- You can play with any of the rolls **once you own** the segmental rolls.

2. Neck Nods

- Perform 10 neck nods.
- On the 5th rep, keep your chin tucked and breathe diaphragmatically 5 times.
- On the 10th rep, keep your chin up, and breathe diaphragmatically 10 times."

3. Rock

- Perform 10 rocks.
- On the last rock, hold the end position (butt to calves) and perform 5 to 10 head nods, raising your head high as if to see over the horizon.

4. Crawl

- Perform 20 baby crawl steps.
- You can substitute army crawling for the baby crawls if you are groggy and want to "wake up".

5. Cross-crawls

- perform 20 cross-crawls anyway you like, slowly.

If you are able, perform this routine three times a day. Why do three resets throughout the day? Why not? All total, they may take 7 to 10 minutes out of your entire day. At worst, they make you move 3 times in a day. At best, they help you become capable of doing anything by solidifying the neural connections that are tied to your foundational patterns. Oh, and they may actually make you smarter!

The Preset

Have you ever seen the movie *Zombie Land*? There is a scene where Woody Harrelson makes fun of his side kick because he starts limbering up in case they encounter zombies while they hunt for Twinkies. Harrelson's character says "You ever seen a lion limber up before taking down a gazelle?" Woody is right. Lions don't limber up, and to be honest, we probably shouldn't have to limber up either. However, we are not lions, nor do we live the lifestyle that lions live. Lions live as lions, the way they were meant to live. We live as rocks, the exact opposite of the way we were meant to live. So, since we live as rocks, it may behoove us to "limber up" a little bit before we engage in a training or playing session.

We call this limber up session a Preset Reset, or simply The Preset. The purpose of the Preset is to simply prepare you for your training session. Regardless of how you train, or what activity or sport you engage in, the Preset will improve your performance.

The Preset is also yet another opportunity to engage in some of our foundational patterns, thus further engraining them in our brains and bodies. If we accumulate enough repetitions of these basic moves on a daily basis, eventually we may end up being more like lions and less like rocks! To be honest, Woody really is right. Life doesn't pause to give us a chance to limber up before the "mess" hits the fan. The more we own our foundational movements, the more capable we are at taking action should we ever need to - the more bulletproof we become.

We really don't care how you train, butwe do care that you perform this Preset before you train. It is *that* important!

The "Preset"

Cross-Crawl x 20 repetitions.
• Perform these slowly.

Segmental Rolls x 3 rolls each limb.
• Who cares how silly you look!

Neck Nods
• 10 reps, slowly.

Rocking x 10 repetitions.
• After the first 5 reps, spread your knees a little further apart and perform 5 more repetitions.

Baby Crawl or Army Crawl x 20 repetitions.

After the "warm-up", engage! Go train, or play, in whatever activity you have planned. Go be a lion. Better yet, be a king or a queen- be a conqueror!

The *Post* Reset

After you train, it is a good idea to Press Reset again. This will not take up a great deal of your time and it may even help you recover faster. Besides, the more you engage in Pressing Reset, the more you will own the patterns and the more efficient your body will become. Here are just a few benefits that a post workout reset can offer.

Your training, or play session, could have been a little too stressful on your body. Let's face it, we don't always pay attention to our bodies, and sometimes we get a little ambitious with our training sessions. We may lift too much, run too far, or turn our head to see what our health club neighbor is wearing while we are squatting. We know, no real "squatter" would get distracted while squatting. But how many of us are actually real "squatters"? Press Reset.

Even with the best focus, sometimes we can *over* stress our brains as well as our bodies. Pressing reset after a training session, or sporting event, can help relax the nervous system and soothe your emotions. There is something very calming and soothing about rolling on the floor and gently rocking back and forth. Press Reset.

If you are like Tim, and your training session is always perfect (he said jokingly), you should still press reset. Maybe you did just the right amount of work and you even hit a personal record. Great, press reset anyway. The purpose of training is to create a stress so that our body has to adapt to that stress, right? *Wouldn't it be cool if you could recover faster and adapt faster too?* <u>Press Reset</u>.

To be repetitious, the last benefit we will point out for the post workout reset is that it simply gives us more repetitions towards engraving our foundational patterns. It is just simple math. The more we perform the resets, the more we own them.

Yes, too much of anything can be a bad thing. That **may** be true. Even if it is, you already sit too much. How many years have you spent sitting down and lying around? Are you worried about that being a bad thing? If not, you should be. Performing resets a few times a day is not going to hurt you. It may help you - a lot. Engraving the resets into our nervous system may eventually cause walking to become the reset it was always meant to be.

The Post Reset

This is not too complicated or time consuming:

March x 20 steps
- Remember to hold your elbows at a 90 degree angle and drive your arms from your shoulders.

Rocking x 5 to 10 repetitions
- If you've had a taxing training session, these will feel good. Spread your knees and open up your hips.

Baby Crawl x 20 steps
- Keep your chest up and "explore" the floor!

Belly Breathing x 3 minutes
- Find your favorite position of comfort and belly breathe. Use that diaphragm!

The Post Reset will not take you long to do, and it is very similar to the Preset Reset. Do it anyway. We are striving to engrain these patterns into your body. That, and Pressing Reset seems to make things work like new again.

Go Outside and Play!

*W*e can learn a lot from watching children and even more from acting like them. This is perhaps the most important concept of this book. Whether or not you believe rolling around on the floor and crawling around like Spider-Man are the miracle resets for your body, you must learn how to play. **We were simply made to move**, and we just don't do what we were designed to do. That is the bottom line.

Do you remember how good you always felt and how much energy you always had as a child? Ever notice how resilient kids are? Do you think we start slowing down and getting injured because we grow old? Or, do you think maybe we grow old and start slowing down because we stop playing? That is definitely something worth pondering.

We need to act more like children. We need to relearn how to play! Ask any kid what his or her favorite part of school is, and he or she will tell you it is recess, the part of the day when they get to go outside and play. That is, of course, at schools where recess is still allowed! We as adults need to learn how to go outside and play. Play can be anything you enjoy doing. It can be a game of basketball, riding a bike, going out for a run, climbing a tree, or anything else you enjoy doing that gets you moving. It doesn't matter what activity you chose for your play session, just **DO SOMETHING!** It can be almost anything as long as you do it. The more fun the better. Just 15 to 30 minutes, it doesn't matter. Just do something - *consistently* (that is the key).

Seriously, go find a playground at a local park, and be a kid! You will be amazed at how good you start to feel. Why? Because you will start using your body the way it was intended. You will start feeling good. You will not only be exercising your body, but also your brain. Maybe you'll relearn some movement patterns, cement some new neural connections in your brain, release some positive hormones in your body, reduce your stress, improve your energy, learn to laugh, etc. The list of benefits just goes on and on.

It's All a Game

Have you ever noticed how a child can turn anything into a game? A child can turn a chore like vacuuming the floor into the Indianapolis 500 Race. Sure, they will probably miss a few spots of the floor, and it may not be as clean as you would like, but they are having fun, learning, playing, and growing. Children simply know how to play. They are masters at creating games and adventures. Why? Because they have imaginations. And more than likely, you don't. The world probably snuffed out your "imagination muscle" a long time ago. This is unfortunate because it is the "imagination muscle" that makes moving and living a fun adventure to be had. The "imagination muscle" makes it possible to turn "work" into "play". If you have lost your imagination muscle you need to get it back. Fortunately for you, like all other muscles, it can be trained and strengthened!

Learning how to be creative and use your imagination, learning how to play, is a crucial step for regaining your original strength. Using your imagination can make all the difference between being able to enjoy moving more than you enjoy watching life pass you by. You must find the kid inside of you and play with joyful movement if you want to overcome the gravity of your couch and the apathy it produces. Be creative and be intentional. Set aside two to three days a week to use your imagination and have fun for 15 to 30 minutes. You can do anything, just make it fun.

For example, Tim is a goof ball. He really still wants to be Superman when he grows up. He's thirty-eight years old, and he has NEVER out-grown that idea. So, when he "plays", he likes to crawl around while pretending to be Spider-Man. (From Tim: I know, I want to be Superman, but I pretend to be Spider-Man - when I'm crawling. When I'm sprinting, I pretend to be Superman.) Anyway, the point is that he's using his imagination and having fun. And, as any kid will tell you, having fun makes moving *fun!*

That is another secret to learning how to play: **FUN!** Playing and having fun are good medicine. They will keep you young and vibrant. I can prove it. When was the last time you played hide-n-seek? I mean, when was the last time you *really* played it? Not with your kids or grandkids, but you played it with people your same size and you played it like you wanted to win? Come on. You know that was your favorite game! Do you remember how fun that was? You could play hide-n-seek for hours! You'd be running as fast as you could, climbing in trees, crawling under bushes, laughing, giggling, snickering, screaming - having the time of your life.

What would happen if, a couple of times a week, you and your neighbors would get together and play hide-n-seek? I know what would happen. You would have fun. You would move your body in all sorts of ways that you would never do being an "adult". You would burn a ton of calories. You would improve your coordination. You would nourish your brain and strengthen your body. You would feel fantastic - *you would feel ALIVE! How awesome would that be?* Can you imagine how good you would feel if you played a good game of hide-n-seek once or twice a week? Will you do it? Will you love your neighbor as yourself? Get them outside and play hide-n-seek! Have fun!

If you are too chicken to play hide-n-seek, you have to learn how to play something; even if it is Hopscotch! What I great game of coordination and a great way to strengthen your legs. You have to learn how to use your imagination and have fun. Create your own games. They *can be anything*, it doesn't really matter what you choose to do. What matters is that you flex your "imagination muscle," **have fun,** and make play a regular part of your life.

Playing Around

Learning how to play may feel weird in the beginning; especially if your imagination muscle has atrophied. Remember, playing can be anything. The most important thing is that it gets you moving and you enjoy it. You have the freedom to be creative and design your own play sessions. You can use your own creativity and do whatever you like. If you are really deconditioned, start out gradually. Maybe set aside ten to fifteen minutes to go outside and play a few times a week. As you start feeling better and more conditioned, increase your time and/or your level of activity. The bottom line is do something, move, and have fun. It really is that simple.

For some of you, having the freedom to explore the idea of playing on your own may be stressful. It need not be. You cannot do this wrong as long as you do something. You really can do anything. Here are some examples:

1. Play dodge-ball with your kids.
2. Go for a walk, or a run, in a park.
3. Go bike riding with some friends. Wear your helmet!
4. Play tennis.
5. Learn how to run sprints.
6. Climb a tree or play on some monkey bars.

7. Learn to swim.

8. Play frisbee golf.

9. Wii yoga!

10. Hide-N-Seek!

Playing may surprise you. You may find that you start enjoying it. You may even find yourself doing things you never thought you would do like signing up for a 5k or joining group bicycle rides. Engaging in play and being active can lead to all sorts of new activities and hobbies. Learning how to play can lead you to a whole new lifestyle. ***Playing can lead to living!***

If the above list did not lower your stress levels and you still feel like you need a little more structure, below are the play session ideas from Mike McNiff, as he laid them out in *Becoming Bulletproof.* Some of these "play sessions" may be seen as full blown workouts. To some people, that is play. Remember, *these are just examples!* Choose the ones you would like to do. Leave the ones you would not want to do. Adjust, change, and tinker with them as you like.

From Mike McNiff as seen in *Becoming Bulletproof*.[50]
The important thing is to do something that gets you moving every day. Modern humans are creatures of habit, but think back to our ancestors. Every day was a new and novel

stimulus. From day to day you never knew whether you would be running from predators, hunting game, migrating, etc. So in order to capitalize on our need for fresh stimulus, our "play dates" should encompass a wide variety of movement. The following are just examples. Feel free to add your own, just remember to have <u>FUN</u>!

1. Every minute on the minute alternate between 5 pull-ups and 10 bodyweight squats. Do this for 20 minutes.

2. Run backwards for 100 steps, drop and do 10 pushups. Side shuffle for 100 steps, drop and do 10 pushups. Skip for 100 steps, drop and do 10 pushups. Run high knees for 100 steps, drop and do 10 pushups. Sprint for 100 steps, drop and do 10 pushups. Repeat as many times as you can in 20 minutes.

3. Find a hill. Sprint up the hill and Spider-Man crawl back down. Repeat five times.

4. Complete the following for time: Do 1 pushup, then 1 burpee. Then 2 pushups, then 2 burpees. Complete that to 10 reps, then start descending back down to 1.

5. Mark off 100 yards. Do as many broad jumps as necessary to reach the end.

6. Do 25 kettlebell swings, then 25 pushups. Then 20 kettlebell swings, then 20 pushups. 15 kettlebell swings, 15 pushups. 10 kettlebell swings, 10 pushups. 5 kettlebell swings, 5 pushups. Complete as many rounds as possible in 20 minutes.

7. Alternate between pull-ups and pushup ladders. Do one pull-up, then one pushup. Add a rep until you can't complete in good form. Then start over at one. Complete as many rounds as possible in 10 minutes.

8. 50 kettlebell swings, then sprint 50 yards. Walk back. Complete 5 times.

9. Sprint 10 yards, jog back. Sprint 20 yards, jog back. Sprint 30 yards, jog back. Sprint 40 yards, jog back. Sprint 50 yards, jog back. Complete twice.

10. Skip rope for 20 UNBROKEN jumps, then 10 pushups. Add 20 jumps and 10 pushups each round. Complete this until you have 100 jumps and 50 pushups.

11. Spider-Man crawl for 100 yards.

12. Summersault 10 times, baby crawl 10 yards, Spider-Man crawl 10 yards, sprint 10 yards, broad jump 10 yards. Complete as many times as you can in 20 minutes.

13. Reverse lunge 15 steps per leg, do 10 pushups, then sprint back to starting point. Repeat 5 times.

14. Do 5 pull-ups or chin-ups, then 10 sit-ups. Keep going until you have done 25 pull/chin ups and 50 sit-ups.

15. Jog a mile.

16. Skip a mile.

17. Skip 100 yards, then backwards run to the start. Do continuously for 10 minutes.

18. Do 5 pushups, then 1 broad jump. 10 pushups, then 1 broad jump. 15 Pushups, then 1 broad jump. 20 pushups, then 1 broad jump. 25 pushups, then 1 broad jump. Complete twice.

19. Do 5 sit ups, then 5 rolls. 5 sit ups, then roll back to start. Do this continuously for 10 minutes.

20. Walk or jog 100 yards, then do 10 pushups. Repeat until you have done 100 pushups.

Joyful Exploration

Before we leave this section on play, here is a question: *Can you see the world through a child's eyes?*

Children approach the world through joyful exploration. Everything they do, everything they discover, is a new adventure. You can actually see the twinkle of excitement in their eyes as they explore their world. It is this joy exploration that also feeds their movement, strengthens their bodies, develops their brains, and makes life fun. If you don't believe me, just give a 2 toddler some wrapping paper, or a ball. You will have made their entire *moment*. We say that because children know how to make moments last and we have lost our ability to savor a day, much less a moment. That is another whole other topic, but it is true.

Anyway, children can be consumed with wonderful fascination over the simplest things in the world. For children, moving, learning and joy are not separate. Every move they make is an act of learning and developing. Every move they make is an act of joy and discovery. We need to learn how to get back to that state - the state where we embrace movement for the sure joy of being able to move. The place where we get excited again and say, "Did you see that? Did you see what I just did? Watch me do it again!!!"

Movement is truly the essence of life. *Especially joyful movement.* Do you remember when the whole world was a playground? Do you remember how it felt the first time you learned you could climb a tree? How it felt when you jumped over your first mud puddle? How it felt when you jumped *in* your first mud puddle? Moving used to be a form of play for you, a form of exploration. We need to get back to the place where we find the joy in moving, discovering, and exploring. Movement is a gift that is meant to be cherished. Children know this. We have forgotten it.

It is time to explore your world through the eyes of a child. Learn how to play and create adventures. Go for hikes in the woods, up mountain sides, or even in a city park. Search for butterflies to catch, mud puddles to jump, trees to climb. Be an explorer, a conqueror, an adventurer. Be a big kid. It will keep you young, healthy, vibrant and joyful. In other words, it will help you regain your original strength.

Teaching Kids to Sit

*H*ave you ever noticed that you have to teach a child how to sit down in a chair? Think about this because it is true. Children have to be taught to sit in chairs. At first, the chairs even have restraining bars to keep the kid from escaping! We use the high chair, or the "safety seat" to keep the child seated and restrained. Have you ever noticed how much a child will fight to keep from being put into one of these chairs? They put up a good fight; until their will is defeated at least. Children just *know* that they don't belong in chairs. It goes against their nature! They want to move, to live.

The wisdom of a child is so beautifully simple that we miss it. We really need to pay attention to how we grow and develop if we want to retain our original strength and youth as we grow older. For example, children intuitively know that they were not made for chairs. So, as *knowing* adults, we teach, force, or convince children to override there intuitive knowledge by requiring them to spend long periods of time in a chair. They fidget, we say sit still. They try to escape, we threaten them. After all, we (adults) know best. But we don't. We are blind. We can see how life happens, how life was meant to be lived by watching our children grow and develop, but yet we dismiss it. We are too busy being smart and sedentary. Children know the secret to health: Movement. We were made to move. We simply were not made to fill up the empty space inside of a chair.

Not only do children know that we were not made for chairs, they also know that chairs were made for us. Have you ever watched a child explore a chair? A chair is an adventure waiting to be conquered. It is a climbing gym, a monkey bar set, a mountain that must be scaled. Even at the ages of 8 and 10, Tim's children think that chairs and couches are parkor obstacles. They know that chairs are better for performing gymnastics and stunts than they are for sitting still in.

It is time to open our eyes. When it comes to moving, to living, we need to pay more attention to our kids. We need to pay more attention to our bodies too. Your body knows that it was not made to sit all day in a chair and it tells you. How do you feel when you get out of a car after a 3 to 4 hour drive? Do you feel like you could run down a gazelle? Or do you feel like you are stiff and "old". Why do you feel so horrible? Because you haven't been moving! We learn this lesson when we get stuck in a car or plane for long periods of time, yet we forget about it on any given day when we purposefully seek out comfortable chairs and couches to spend several hours in. Sitting in chairs for long periods of time from day to day robs you of your original strength. It weakens your body. It weakens your brain. It shortens you lifespan.

If there is one tip in this whole book that could change and improve your life forever, it would be this: Get out of the chair and get back down on the floor. Move, and sit, like children do. Watch how a child sits on the floor. When a child sits, his muscles are engaged, his body is using strength in a "resting" position. His spinal stabilizers are working. Conversely, when an adult sits, or "melts", into a chair, his muscles are no longer engaged. In fact, the body is just being supported more by facia and skin than it is by bone structure and muscle. Literally, when we sit in chairs for long periods of time, we become sacks of flesh.

But not a child! When a child sits on the floor, in all of the hundreds of positions that they do, they are still "strength training". They are still using their bodies' intended design. In a sense, when a child is sitting still on the floor, he is actually moving.

Weird, but true - because his body is engaged! Guess what? If you get down on the floor and learn how to move, AND actually learn how to sit again, or "rest" on the floor, you will regain your body's strength and mobility. Spend some time learning how to get comfortable while sitting, and being, on the floor. Learn how to easily move from one position to another.

Even if you don't perform the resets outlined in this book, though we can't imagine why you wouldn't, spending time on the floor can change your life. Not only will it help you regain some of your strength and mobility, you will discover a very important life skill: How to get up from the floor!

Think about it, the more ways that you can get up from the floor, the healthier and more resilient you will be. As a matter of fact, that is not a bad game for you to play every other day or so: How many different ways can I get up from the ground in 10 minutes? This simple, *ridiculously simple,* game can make the difference between living independently in your 80's or occupying a rest-home bed in your 70's.

Here is how you play: Get down on the floor! Learn how to sit in all kinds of positions. Learn to go from crawling to sitting, from sitting to crawling, to standing. Learn how to flow from one to the other. How seamless can you flow in and out from rolling, crawling, kneeling, standing? How many different ways can you do this? How many different ways can you learn to stand without using your hands? Just play! Use your imagination, design strategies and techniques to move and get up. When you can flow from one position to another with grace, congratulations! You are strong! And, you have just added years of quality life to your body.

This simple game, is a great way to nourish both your brain and your body. It gets you thinking about movement, movement strategy, and it gets you moving! It enables you to regain strength, stamina and energy. Don't believe us? Try it. You will probably be out of breath in less than three minutes - though you will enjoy the process. Maybe - eventually.

If you are blessed enough to have small children now, learn from them. Watch them learn to move and move to learn as they grow. Notice how they are always moving in some way, how they intuitively know when to rest after they struggle with a new move or obstacle. Get down on the floor and move with them. Crawl with them, roll with them. Climb over the backs of chairs with them. Learn to find the healing, restorative, joy of moving like a child. Whatever you do, if you want to enjoy life into a ripe old age, get out of that chair. You were never meant to be a sack of flesh.

Strength Training

*S*trength training can also play a pivotal role in regaining your original strength. We don't know of anyone who could not benefit from getting stronger. Having strength is like having armor. It can protect you from unfortunate injuries, and it can enable you to perform unusual tasks. Strength makes you resilient.

In 1989, Dr. Phillip Maffetone wrote a book called *In Fitness and In Health: Everyone is an Athlete.* We love this concept. We love it because deep down, we know it is true. Think about it. **You are an athlete.** <u>You were made to move</u>. You were perfectly designed in every way.

We are all athletes. Therefore, we should all train like athletes. A professional athlete usually strength trains no more than twice a week during the season of their sport. The rest of their week, they practice their sport and their skills and then they play their sport. One day when Tim was talking to our friend, Mike McNiff, about our ideas on training, he said one of the most brilliant things we have ever heard. *"**You should train the way an elite athlete trains for their sport. Your sport is life**."*[51] That is an awesome statement! Our sport is life and we should be prepared for it.

Here is our training plan to prepare you for the "Sport of Life" and whatever it throws at you.

Strength train twice a week. Then, PLAY (do something) the rest of the week. Earth shattering we know. But, it works. It works for elite athletes, and it will work for you. Best of all, it is **SIMPLE**.

If you are new to the idea of strength training, it may be a good idea to start strength training by learning how to move your own body and use your own bodyweight. You can develop really good levels of strength and a great physique just by learning how to use your own body.

Remember the lowly pushup? It is a tremendous whole body strength developer! A perfect pushup requires strength! Is a perfect pushup too challenging for you? Start Spider-Man crawling! You will develop the strength you need to perform the pushup. Yes, even crawling can be strength training.

If you are a beginner, we think it is a really good idea to learn how to do a few basic moves to help you get started.

The mighty pushup!

The incline pushup

- Learn how to do a pushup. If you can't do one on the floor, learn how to do them from an incline position or from your knees.
- Learn how to squat. Squatting is a pattern you once had as a child, and it is a pattern you need to keep.

The bodyweight squat

The assisted squat using a strap

The following program is a *simple* strength training program for **beginners**. It can be done by almost anyone, and it will get you stronger and ready for more challenging exercises:

First, pick two days a week to strength train, like maybe Monday and Thursday or Tuesday and Saturday. Just pick two days with ample recovery time in between them.

Days 1 and 2:
Warm-up by pressing reset.
Perform 5 perfect pushups for 5 sets
Perform 10 bodyweight squats for 5 sets
Spider-man crawl for 3 minutes - if you have to rest, rest. But try for a total crawl-time of 3 minutes.

Each week, try to add another set to your pushups and squats until you are able to perform 20 sets of 5 pushups and 10 sets of 10 squats for a total of 100 each. Also, once you can perform the spider-man crawl for a continuous 3 minutes, start adding 30 seconds of crawl-time each week until you can crawl for 5 minutes.

Once you have accomplished this, it is time to change it up just a little:

Days 1 and 2:

Warm-up by pressing reset.

Perform 10 perfect pushups for 5 sets

Perform 20 bodyweight squats for 5 sets

Spider-man crawl backwards for 3 minutes - if you have to rest, rest. But try for a total crawl-time of 3 minutes.

Each week, try to add another set to your pushups and squats until you are able to perform 10 sets of 10 pushups and 10 sets of 20 squats. Also, once you can perform the backwards Spider-Man crawl for a continuous 3 minutes, start adding 30 seconds of crawl-time each week until you can crawl for 5 minutes.

Once you have accomplished this, congratulations! You are stronger and you are now ready to explore more levels of strength training.

Reset Your Training

Please keep in mind the above strength training program was for beginners; for people who just need a place to start. There are many, MANY ways and methods to train for strength and health - with some being better than others. However, it doesn't matter what form of strength training you subscribe to, pressing reset before, during, and after your training sessions WILL make your training sessions more effective. In other words, you can reset your strength training to become faster, stronger and more powerful.

Think about this: To be fast, strong, and powerful you need to be able to relax. A stressed out, tight body is a body that is stiff, slow, and rigid. A stiff, slow and rigid body is a body that has a higher chance of being injured. Two great minds, Bud Winter and Pavel Tsatsouline, have both preached the importance of staying relaxed and fast and loose, respectively, when it comes to performance.

It is arguable that Bud Winter has had the greatest impact in the sport of track and field than any other coach in history. His coaching and relaxation techniques helped produce

37 world record holders, 27 Olympians, and 102 NCAA All-Americans.[52] In WWII, Bud was even called upon by the military to teach US fighter pilots his techniques for relaxation so they could quickly distinguish the difference between friends or foes while in combat![53] There is no question, relaxation is crucial for performance.

Pavel Tsatsouline teaches his concept of "fast and loose" to enable athletes and combatants the ability to relax and rejuvenate their bodies to help improve their performance. Pavel often states that elite athletes are masters at relaxation and he himself has demonstrated time and time again that a relaxed body is a powerful body.

A relaxed body is a body that can move well. Both Bud Winter's and Pavel's techniques work very well for relieving tension and improving performance. However, their techniques are skills; skills that come with a learning curve. It may be no surprise to you that *pressing reset* is another method, perhaps even a better method, that can relax, or reset, the body and improve performance.

It can be hard to teach someone how to relax and "shake" their muscles loose. It can be hard for people to learn how to clear their minds and just "let go." However, almost anyone can be taught how to march, or rock on the floor, or roll. Pressing reset can instantly relax the nervous system, and thus the body, enabling you to move and perform better. Best of all, the learning curve is pretty minimal.

To illustrate the power of pressing reset, let's look at strength training. Performing resistance exercise increases tension in the muscles and stress in the nervous system. Take squatting for example: after a set of heavy squats, the body is a little more tight, tired and stressed. Once the body is stressed, it can be hard to perform consecutive sets with the same focus, energy, and strength that was applied to the first "heavy" set. What if you could just press a reset button and restore the body's nervous system back to a relaxed and ready state, thus enabling you to perform well on your next set? What if you could instantly refresh your body and improve your movements while under the stress of added load? You can. And, it is pretty easy to do. It's as easy as marching in place.

If you strength train, you should be training to get strong in a safe and effective manner. Your goal should be to have strength so that you can enjoy your life and / or perform well at your sport. Even if you treat strength training as your sport, you would probably agree that in order for you to be happy, you need to be able to train. So it would only makes sense that your strength training routine should be built around quality movements and not merely the quantity of movements. Here is where pressing reset really comes into play.

Pressing reset between your strength training sets can really help to revive the body and clean up any movement deterioration caused by the stress of strength training itself. In other words, if you reset yourself between sets, you will move better longer and improve the quality of your training. The better you move while under a load, the less chance you have for an injury and the more resilient you will become because you are adding strength to a solid movement foundation. Simply put, pressing reset while you train can relax your nervous system and improve your strength, speed, power, and focus. Your quality of movement stays up and your risk of injury stays low.

Try this yourself. Take a weight that you struggle to press one to two times and press it. Then get on the floor and rock back and forth five to ten times. Now press your weight again. You may find that the weight went up easier, and you were able to press it more than you did the first time. Pressing reset simply works.

When it comes to strength training, or training in general, we like to combine certain resets with certain movements.

From Tim: If my movements are fast, like a kettlebell swing, I like to perform slower resets, like rocking, in between sets. If my movements are slow, like a heavy front squat, I like to perform faster moving resets like marching. I also like the idea of performing rolls after spinal compression caused from exercises like back squats or deadlifts.

From Geoff: I like to use resets that enhance my movements. For example, if I'm squatting or doing some sort of kettlebell ballistic, I'll probably do some sort of rocking or crawling. And some days, I'll perform a ton of neck nods and rocking especially if I've been in front of the computer a lot. At the end of the day there is no "one" sequence I use. I have learned to listen to the feedback my body gives me and choose my resets based on that feedback.

There are no rules though. You can perform the reset you feel you need. But just to give you some ideas, we'll show you some examples here:

Movement Resets

- Swings x 10 to 20 reps, followed by rocking x 5 to 10 reps
- Goblet Squats x 3 to 5 reps, followed by marching x 20 steps
- Back squats x 3 to 5 reps, followed by elevated rolls x 2 rolls each leg
- Clean and press x 3 to 5 reps, followed by rocking x 5 to 10 reps
- Strict overhead presses x 3 to 5 reps, followed by marching or cross-crawls x 20 steps
- Heavy Deadlifts (I know, is there any other kind of deadlift?) x 1 to 3 reps, followed by elevated rolls x 2 rolls each leg
- Sprinting x 60 yards, followed by rocking x 5 to 10 reps
- Pull-ups x 5 to 10 reps, followed by hard rolls x 2 rolls each way
- Olympic Lifts (you pick!) x 1 to 3 reps, followed by rocking x 5 to 10 reps

Again, there are no rules here. Experiment with the resets and use the ones that tend to relax you and restore you the most. You may be pleasantly surprised to find that your movements get better and better as you train, and you end your training sessions feeling refreshed and invigorated. That should be the point!

Traditional Training Templates - For those of you who are "in the box" thinkers!

Admittedly, some of you, like Geoff, may not be ready to just go out and play like we suggested earlier. Or you may just not want to. You may be fascinated with traditional forms of strength training. And that's fine.

Here are some strength training program templates you can use that integrate Original Strength principles and resets.

<u>3 Days A Week</u>

Day 1: Reset, Barbell Strength Work, Conditioning, Reset
Day 2: Reset, Barbell Strength Work, Conditioning, Reset
Day 3: Reset, Barbell Strength Work, Conditioning, Reset

*Substitute Barbell with Kettlebell, Dumbbell, Bodyweight, or whatever

<u>4 Days A Week</u>

Day 1: Reset, Barbell Strength Work, Reset
Day 2: Reset, Conditioning, Reset
Day 3: Reset, Barbell Strength Work, Reset

Day 4: Reset, Conditioning, Reset

5 Days A Week

Day 1: Reset, Barbell Strength Work, Reset

Day 2: Reset, Conditioning, Reset

Day 3: Reset, Barbell Strength Work, Reset

Day 4: Reset, Conditioning, Reset

Day 5: Reset, Barbell Strength, Reset

6 Days A Week

Day 1: Reset, Barbell Strength Work, Reset

Day 2: Reset, Conditioning, Reset

Day 3: Reset, Barbell Strength Work, Reset

Day 4: Reset, Conditioning, Reset

Day 5: Reset, Barbell Strength, Reset

Day 6: Reset, Conditioning, Reset

Combining Modalities With Original Strength Workouts

3 Days A Week

Workout A: Traditional Strength

Workout B: OS Resets like Crawling

Alternate on non-consecutive days between Workout A and Workout B.

   Monday: Workout A

   Wednesday: Workout B

   Friday: Workout A

   Monday: Workout B

   Wednesday: Workout A

   Friday: Workout A

4 Days A Week

Workout A: Traditional Strength

Workout B: OS Resets like Crawling

   Monday: Workout A

   Tuesday: Workout B

   Thursday: Workout A

   Friday / Saturday: Workout B

5 Days A Week

Workout A: Traditional Strength

Workout B: OS Resets like Crawling

Monday: Workout A

Tuesday: Workout B

Wednesday: Workout A

Thursday: Workout B

Friday: Workout A

6 Days A Week

Workout A: Traditional Strength

Workout B: OS Resets like Crawling

Monday: Workout A

Tuesday: Workout B

Wednesday: Workout A

Thursday: Workout B

Friday: Workout A

Saturday: Workout B

Other Ideas

3 Days / 6 Days A Week

Day 1: Barbell Strength

Day 2: Bodyweight Strength

Day 3: Original Strength

(Repeat Days 1 through 3 on days 4 through 6.)

Sample:

Monday: Military Press, Front Squat

Wednesday: Chins, Parallel Dips, Pistols

Friday: Leopard Crawls for distance

Day 1: Kettlebell Strength

Day 2: Bodyweight Strength

Day 3: Original Strength

Sample:

Monday: Get Up, Swing, Press

Wednesday: Chins, Parallel Dips, Pistols

Friday: Leopard Crawls for time

4 Days A Week

Day 1: Barbell and Kettlebell

Day 2: Bodyweight and Original Strength

Day 3: Barbell and Kettlebell

Day 4: Bodyweight and Original Strength

Sample:

Monday: Military Press, Front Squat, Swings

Tuesday: Chins, Dips, Crawling

Thursday: Deadlift, Bench Press, Swings

Friday / Saturday: Handstand Push ups, Pistols, Crawling

5 Days A Week

Day 1: Barbell

Day 2: Original Strength

Day 3: Bodyweight

Day 4: Original Strength

Day 5: Kettlebell

Sample:

Monday: Deadlift, Military Press, Front Squat

Tuesday: Crawling

Wednesday: Chins, Handstand Push Ups, Pistols

Thursday: Crawling

Friday: Get Ups, Swings, Goblet Squats

Outside The Box: *True* Original Strength Training

The beautiful thing about the Original Strength System is its simplicity. It refreshes your body's original operating system with easy to do, already done variations of the way you developed as a kid. The only difference today is that when you were a baby, you had a big old head that you used as resistance. Today, we don't. So we introduce duration and a little bit of complexity. Not a lot - just a little bit.

Anytime, Anywhere Workouts

I (Geoff) do a lot of traveling. Since I like to work out (train) every day, one of the best ways to stay in shape while in hotels is to crawl.

I have two standby workouts:

Spiderman crawling down the hallways either early in the morning or late at night. Or when I'm feeling particularly tired, I'll put on a podcast and do Baby crawls back and forth in my room for 10 minutes non-stop.

I feel amazingly rejuvenated and always sleep well afterwards.

Obviously, you can do this at home. Having a big backyard helps. Parks work well too.

We use one of the crawls: Baby, Leopard, or Spiderman.

Why?

Because as an infant, crawling was one of the predominant activities you used to gain your strength to be able to walk, and later run.

How do we do it?

We crawl for time. We crawl for steps. We crawl in different directions - backwards and side-to-side.

Now, here, as Shakespeare said, is the rub: *This is ALL we do*.

We know this sounds crazy, but when you can crawl 100 yards non-stop, keeping your head up, you've done something, and you know it, especially if it's a Spider-man crawl!

When you really want to see *ah-mazing* results, plan on doing some kind of crawling every day - 6 days a week.

Doing this, Geoff was able to get his bodyweight Pistol (one-legged rock bottom squat) and his One Arm One Leg Push Up (OAOLPU). And Tim would never tell you this, so Geoff will: From some specialized crawling, Tim did (and captured on video) a barbell Turkish Get Up with 135 pounds on each side, at a bodyweight of 153 pounds. *That's some **serious** strength!*

Ideas For True Original Strength Training

- Leopard crawl for 100 yards/meters. Repeat 4 to 8 times. (Yes, that's between 1/4 and a 1/2 mile!)
- Spiderman crawl for 5 minutes without stopping.
- Baby crawl for 10 minutes without stopping.
- Backwards crawling for 20 steps per leg. Repeat.
- Lateral crawling 30 yards at a clip.
- Mix and match.
- See how long it takes you to crawl a 1/4 mile, a 1/2 mile, or a mile.

All Out = Full On (The Only Time Failure Equals Success)

When you watch a baby or toddler or even a younger child play, they never do anything to failure. Sure, they may try something two or three times, like picking something heavy up off the floor, but they won't overly strain to do so. They won't use "intensity" techniques, go into the zone, or get psyched up. They either can do it without psyching up, or they don't do it at all.

Today, we know this is scientifically validated - training to failure places the central nervous system under undue stress. The only thing - or only exercise that I've seen that can be trained to failure, to utter exhaustion, and you can come back the next day and do it all over again without experiencing CNS fatigue - is Crawling.

Of course it's dependent on what level of crawling you can do. But nonetheless, you can crawl, hard, every day, and still see positive daily results.

The 800 Pound Gorilla
In The Room

*W*e've all experienced the 800 pound gorilla at some point or another - you know that big somewhat menacing thing that everyone knew existed but no one dared say anything about - yeah, *that* thing.

Well it seems to me that there's an 800 pound gorilla we're skirting around here - Mobility.

Actually, *mobility and stability* - their roles in our training, and their roles within Original Strength.

We are not big fans of mobility work - or at least not the way it's often promoted or prescribed today. And that's because we have both done our fair share of it: Geoff did it almost incessantly for four years - multiple times per day, and Tim did it for an almost similar period of time. And we used it with our clients. Geoff's wife, a Doctor of Physical Therapy used it with herself and her patients, and so did several of our friends, who are also fitness professionals. The unfortunate thing was that nothing good came of it *in the long term*.

Here's a question for you: *Why do you think a joint becomes immobile?*

The most obvious answer would be "lack of use."

Therefore, we naturally think, let's pry that joint back open so we can use it again and reintegrate it into the body.

But what if that's the wrong conclusion? What if we need to dig a little deeper - look a little more closely in another area - perhaps an area that requires some non-linear thinking?

Here's where this gets even more interesting: There have been several times where we have seen either in private sessions or in seminars where people have increased ankle mobility without mobilizing their ankles (or wrists or feet or hands, if you've been involved in some of the programs we've been involved with). In fact, the common theme has been head movement - and head/neck control. Increased head and neck movement (and subsequent control) has increased ankle mobility.

What's going on? How does that happen? Well before we get there, let's go back and take a closer look at this whole mobility-stability thing.

Some have proposed a "mobility-stability continuum" - that certain joints require more stability and others more mobility, where the following definitions apply:

Stability: The ability to resist an undesired movement

Mobility: The ability to produce a desired movement (Hartman)

For example, the knee needs more stability while the thoracic spine needs more mobility. While we think those are very good definitions, we think they are lacking one thing:

Context.

Let's take a closer look.

The "mobility-stability continuum" is a reductionist approach, that is to say, one that looks at what's going on with pieces, parts, and not the whole, which is commonly referred to as an empirical approach.

This gets us back to looking at these concepts from a different view point or perspective - or the empirical approach. What if excess mobility - or hypermobility - like we often see in the lumbar spine and lower cervical spine is really the same symptom as excess stability (immobility) that we often see in the ankles and thoracic spine?

Based on our work with our clients and patients, we believe that mobility and stability are indeed a continuum as some suggest, but they are a *symptomatic continuum* of a greater problem to be addressed.

In other words, the joint-by-joint approach of assessing and addressing mobility and stability is flawed because it is treating symptoms - the symptoms of immobility and hypermobility - instead of treating the problem, the root cause.

The Root Cause _AND_ The Solution: Reflexive Stability and Strength

Geoff is blessed at the time of this writing with a 23 month old son. Part of our Original Strength journey has been him watching, observing, ascertaining, and mimicking his son's developmental sequence. This has become the backbone of our regressions that we teach in our workshops.

From the day he was born (conceived really) his body was pre-programmed to get him to where he is right now - running around upright on two feet. And he's still not fully developed. He has about another year or so to go.

What has enabled him to get to upright was what we call the developmental movement sequence, which is what Original Strength (OS) is based off. (Anyone notice that the initials OS also stand for "Operating System?" Interesting. . .)

And this developmental movement sequence builds what is called **reflexive stability** or **reflexive strength**.

As the word reflexive indicates, this is a strength that is automatic and beyond the control of your conscious mind. It is hardwired into your central nervous system and literally every cell in your body. It's the strength that allows you to move without having to think about moving. And when you do have to think about moving, that's a telltale sign that your reflexive strength is missing.

In simplest terms, your reflexive stability / reflexive strength is your body's ability to automatically anticipate and control movement - contracting the right muscles at the right times in the right orders with the right force enabling the right joints to move to accomplish whatever task you are attempting to do.

Geoff's son does not think about movement. He just moves. Or not. If he can't move one way, he moves another.

<u>And that's a critical point</u>: As an infant and toddler this is part of his growth process - part of his ability to gain his reflexive strength. As adults, this is part of survival and we call these "other movements" **compensations**. And these compensations are what cause our soft tissue issues, like trigger points and our non-contact joint injuries. More on them in a minute.

So what does all this have to do with mobility and stability?

As I said, we don't do "mobility work." Nor do we do "stability" work. Immobility (too much stability) and hypermobility (not enough stability) are both symptoms of the same root problem:

Loss of reflexive stability / reflexive strength.

The reason our bodies lose mobility or create excess mobility is that we've lost some of our reflexive stability and strength. So we are not able to move as effortlessly as we were created.

And therefore our bodies, in their intuitive wisdom and their survival program, compensate. The body, subconsciously and automatically redirects its energy away from things that were created to move to things that weren't, or things that were created to move a lot to things that were only created to move a little. So we end up with hips that are tight, and lower backs that are loose. And then, we load them with a barbell across the back or a kettlebell in the hands. And maybe even put wedges under our heels to make up for that lack of "mobility." And then the injury cycle begins. . .

So how do we regain that joint mobility and stability? Before I answer that, let's take a closer look to why we end up with immobile/hyper-stabile joints in the first place.

Ever see a toddler walk?

It's hilarious and always puts a smile on Geoff's face. Toddlers walk with their feet apart, and not together. And they kind of zig-zag - bounce back and forth off each foot to create forward momentum. Why is that?

Because they haven't fully developed their reflexive stability and strength. And they haven't developed it in their "core" - their midsection, the crossroads of locomotion and efficient force transfer.

And when the fall, they almost bounce. This is because they are incredibly mobile - not hypermobile - just mobile. Sure, they may take some skin off their knee and cry a little bit, but within moments, with just a mild amount of distraction, they're off running around again, bouncing back and forth, exploring their environment.

By contrast, you ever seen a frail old person walk?

It's almost the same way. They walk with a wide stance just like a toddler - but without the lateral bounce. It's more of a shuffle.

When an elderly person falls, the results are much more severe than a toddler's fall. These falls often end up with severe trauma - like broken bones and joint replacements, and in many cases, like a broken hip, with death not too far behind.

What's the difference?

Well an elderly person has lost his or her reflexive stability and strength and the body has literally splinted the joints, by contracting the muscles, in order to prevent movement. (And obviously an older person has greater mass that falls a greater distance. But a baby or toddler has his big melon head to keep from smashing into the ground and that's a lot of work too.)

Hold on, that "joint splinting" looks familiar, doesn't it? What's going on here?

Toddlers vs. Experts

Geoff's son doesn't stretch. He doesn't even know what the word means. Nor does he perform self-myofascial release on his baby foam roller. (He doesn't have one.) And he doesn't warm up to for any activity or event: Not running, not pushing his truck or his stroller, not when he hangs from the bar in the park. Nope. None of it. Ever. Nor does he use a stick to roll out tight spots, adhesions, or a Thera-cane for trigger points.

We know, we know, he doesn't have your "mileage" does he.

But he has something that you don't have - a big head. And that melon is the way he strength trains. It's his own portable gym. That's how he gets his reflexive strength and his reflexive stability and why he doesn't have to warm up.

In case you're not following us, because his head is bigger in relationship to his body than yours, his vestibular system is constantly being stimulated, and therefore so is his reflexive strength - he is gaining and training his Original Strength.

We know you may be scratching your head and wondering what this has to do with stretching, muscle splinting, and mobility and stability.

Here's the punchline:

1. Lack of mobility is due to lack of reflexive stability/ reflexive strength.
2. Lack of stability is due lack of reflexive strength.
3. Unnecessary muscle stiffness or tightness is because of a loss of reflexive strength.
4. Movement compensations are due to a loss of reflexive strength.

Therefore, when you understand that your problems are really just symptoms, and you address the root cause of those symptoms, your loss of reflexive stability and strength, you will automatically restore your body's natural strength, its Original Strength, its natural operating system, and many if not all of these symptoms will correct themselves.

Over the course of time, there is no longer a need for things like self-myofascial release, trigger point therapy, joint mobility training, or stretching. How much time? Depends on how long you've had those issues. We have seen results in many cases become immediate and permanent. Why and how? Because we're not correcting or changing anything here - we are refreshing, restoring your body to the way it was designed to be - think natural instead of normal.

There now, that gorilla doesn't seem so big anymore does he? Looks more like one of those little monkeys you see in the circus selling peanuts, huh?

The Fallacy of Neutral Spine And The Rise of "Artificial Neutral"

(Adapted from Geoff's, *"Kettlebell STRONG!"* book.)

O ver the last 6 or so years, there's been a lot of contro- versy on the position of the head when lifting weights.

Is it the traditional eyes forward, head up? Or is it neck neutral / neck packed?

Before I give you my answer, let's consider how the body is designed. When your body is operating correctly, your eyes lead the way. You already know for example, when you look up, your body moves ever so slightly into extension (leans back). And when you look down, your body moves ever so slightly into flexion (leans forward). These are reflexes that are hardwired into you and which are developed during the first couple months after birth. You continue to "cement" these reflexes until about the age of three.

Also consider, that based on these extension and flexor reflexes, the natural order of movement is:

- The eyes lead
- The head follows the eyes
- The body follows the head

An argument has been made (which I bought into around 2006) that the head and neck should remain in neutral when lifting. The rationale is that this preserved the natural curves of the spine and allowed the joints of the spine to be centrated and therefore more neural drive ("nerve force") made it to the muscles, allowing for stronger muscular actions.

This sounded great in theory and pro- duced some fairly positive results in the short run.

The problem with this theory is that it ignores the body's natural and normally hardwired reflexes that we discussed earlier.

181

So as soon as you bend over and load the body your reflexes should naturally operate. One of those reflexes, the Righting Reflex, is an *automatic reflex* to bring the head back over the body's base of support and the head in line with the horizon. (There are actually several Righting Reflexes.)

I want to emphasize here that this is a ***natural and hardwired reaction***. To train in "long spine" or with a "packed neck" for the sake of joint centration or supposed increased neural drive, <u>trains your body out of this reflex</u>.

How?

Because part of the righting reflexes responses is when you bend forward (flexion), your body automatically fires off the extensor reflexes to control/prevent you from collapsing against the weight of gravity. And when you move into extension, such as a back bend, your body automatically fires off the flexor reflexes to keep gravity from collapsing your spine.

Here is a perfect example caught in this picture of Maurice Deriaz, the great Swiss strongman, performing a one-arm Clean & Jerk with 228 pounds.

Notice how his spine is naturally forming an arch (one of the strongest structures known to man) to support the load.

The spine naturally curves toward the direction of the load unless you cognitively / consciously override it. So, when you bend at the waist, such as in deadlifting, your body's natural and normal reaction is to arch the spine toward the load, forming an arch, from that position – from flexion into extension. This too is a reflex: The the body automatically compresses, or "zips up," as Pavel teaches in his book, The Naked Warrior." I've seen this with my son, as early as 18 months old when he picks something off the floor or if he feels like I'm going to lower him from my arms. The muscles of the body move toward the center of the body.

Therefore if you continually seek "axial extension" or to "pack your neck" you are training aberrant and unnatural movement patterns and are essentially fighting and potentially dulling your reflexes. This increases your injury potential.

183

Are you sure you want to do that?

(I am aware of the argument that some elite level powerlifters use some variations of neck packing and possibly even axial extension. But they are very few and they are not the norm. So basing your strategies on a few outliers in a fringe competition is not a smart idea for long term health and performance.)

What About Neutral Spine – Shouldn't You Maintain That Under Load?

That's a great question.

My answer is "what do you say neutral spine is?"

I question the wisdom and logic of trying to maintain the body's natural curves while standing while in other positions.

Because they're just that – neutral, and therefore natural, _while standing_.

As soon as you move the body, various reflexes (righting, pneumomuscular, etc), based on positioning and load, are initiated. I think the faulty logic we have used is that under load those curves should be maintained as they are while standing.

184

If that were the case, then spine wouldn't be as articulated as it is and wouldn't be the perfect shape for bipedal locomotion – our primary "function."

Think about this:

When you bend forward at the waist or hinge at the hips for a Swing or a Deadlift, we are making an assumption that "neutral" is the maintained the same way as it is standing, so the cue "long spine."

But when you bend over, as I mentioned earlier, your "righting reflexes" are initiated and they're designed to keep your head over your body and your eyes level with the horizon – an internal gyroscope if you will, unless you are willfully overriding them, like squatting down to look at something on the ground, like my little boy will often do. Even then, your reflexes are at work, making sure your body is perfectly counterbalanced.

Normal v. Natural

Many of us confuse normal with natural. *Normal* is what you're used to doing, what feels right. *Natural* is what you're designed to do, what you're supposed to do, and may feel awkward when you first start doing it again. The more you perform resets, the more natural becomes your new normal.

For example: If you look down at the ground in a squat for example, your body naturally shifts backwards, displacing your center of mass over the back of your feet into your heels, and your shins will start to become vertical. From that same position, if you look up, your body naturally shifts your weight forward into your mid-foot, even your toes, to maintain its center of gravity over its base of support. If it did not, you'd lose your balance and fall backwards.

(Incidentally, this is one of the reasons many people can't squat today. Their reflexes have been "dulled" and they no longer work automatically as they should. More on that shortly. . .)

The obvious next question is, *does this change with load?*

The answer is "yes."

Depending on where the load is, the body should naturally change its positioning to counterbalance that load.

For example, when the weight is in the hands, the center of mass is pulled forward. The body naturally counterbalances the load by reflexively activating its extensors, specifically the posterior chain. (It also reflexively holds the breath, compresses the viscera and braces the spine through intra-abdominal pressure - the valsalva maneuver and pneumomuscular reflex.)

And since the body is designed to follow the head, and the head the eyes, naturally and normally the head will be up, or slightly up, with the neck in extension (not hyperextension – don't confuse the two). This is because the "neck-on-body" righting reflex stimulates the extensor muscles to bring the body back to an upright position. Let me say this again in case you missed it the first time: <u>This is a natural and normal reflex</u>.

The same is true for all forms of external loading – the body seeks to support the load through using its reflexes first.

This all begs a very serious question:

Well Why Do People Report Positive Results Using These Strategies?

I'll be the first to admit that I too saw positive results when I first used them too. Why? Because they were new stimuli to the body that provoked a positive short term response. That's it. And those changes are especially noticeable in people with injuries and "high mileage."

I have the good fortune to have trained clients for as long as 11 and-a-half years, so I get to see the body's *long-term responses* to these strategies. <u>And they haven't been good</u>.

Why not?

Because we (the fitness/medical/exercise fields) are operating under the assumption that the keys to "fixing" posture are purely musculoskeletal or purely neuromuscular, that is, we either address the muscles or the "nervous system" and we come up with strategies that appear to address the problems but instead only address the symptoms.

So what IS the problem?

<u>Reflexes</u>.

Quite simply, our reflexes are dulled, from environmental factors, specifically sitting. Address or sharpen the body's natural, normal, and hardwired reflexes, and these issues take care of themselves, with no extra effort on our part.

And that's the purpose of **Original Strength** - to help you sharpen and regain those lost reflexes, and in doing so, restore your original movement patterns, eliminate movement dysfunctions, help you fix aches, pains, and injuries, and help you live the wonderful physical life you were designed and supposed to live.

To sum up, based upon my observation of long term clients, my developing son, and pertinent literature, neutral spine is position-dependent. There are different "neutrals" related to the activity, assuming of course, your reflexes are working correctly.

That may not convince you, so let me tell you some observations I've made both in person and on video from advocates of these various theories:

I've never seen a person keep "packed neck" or neutral neck under high-speed load. And I've seen A LOT of people perform the kettlebell ballistics over the last 10 + years. The head and neck always do either one of two things: fall into flexion or move into extension – there is no middle ground. The closest I've seen to keeping this neutral position is Master SFG Brett Jones, and even he has since reverted back to a "head up" position on his ballistics and as such his performance and health have improved.

Nine times out of ten, the advocates of neck packing fail to maintain a packed neck at the end of the backswing of the KB ballistics. When watching demonstrations – video or still, I see cervical protrusion often times combined with cervical flexion. (The pushing forward of the head combined with the dropping of the chin.) Sometimes it's one or the other. Again, this initiates the body's flexor reflexes – to make the flexor chain contract – which is the exact opposite of what we want to get out of the backswing. We want the extensor chain to work. So at the risk of beating a dead horse here, we want the head up to maintain the body's natural extensor reflexes and avoid any sort of "reflex confusion."

Many "neck packing" and "long spine" advocates finish their ballistics with their heads in flexion instead of on the top of the body. This comes from an unwitting over-reliance on the flexor reflex/ flexor chain. It's a great way to destabilize your lower back and end up with lumbar spine issues down the road. (Ask me how I know. . .)

The body should "unwind" under the head during the backswing of the kettlebell ballistics. This is just what it sounds like – the head stays on top of the body, with some horizontal displacement (obviously) but the spine does not move as one piece. It articulates reflexively in response to the load. Don't worry if you can't imagine it – like a good work of art, you'll know it when you see it.

The assumption is made that joints can't be centrated if the exact spinal curves are not maintained or maintained in relation to each other. If this has not been measured across ALL populations with EMG analysis and fluoroscopy, then this is a best guess, not hard science. Plus, it is also science performed on a population with movement restrictions and joint dysfunctions.

Many people are confusing neck extension with neck *hyperextension*. Many people see neck extension (again, which is a natural movement, even as is hyperextension, even though the latter is not preferable and can be damaging) and automatically shout, "Her neck is hyperextended!" That's not always the case. It's actually quite easy to see and most often happens around C2-C3 and looks like an actual kink – or an angular appearance. As I mentioned earlier, you can't say definitively unless you are looking at movement under a fluoroscope.

Loss of thoracic mobility cannot be compensated for by locking up the neck by packing it or keeping it neutral. Many people have complained of neck pain discomfort while keeping their eyes on the horizon during kettlebell ballistics.

191

Neck packing anecdotally alleviates their pain, which of course, is awesome. However, neck issues are often because of a lack of mobility in the thoracic spine. So unless you have full range of motion in your T-spine, you are most likely just addressing your symptoms and masking the root cause of the problem.

The argument that ontologically (developmentally) the neck should be kept packed under load for safety reasons is flawed. The argument for "neck packing" under load is supposedly because the neck is a structure that's designed for quick, unloaded movements. This argument based solely on its structure assumes that force is being absorbed by the neck structures (loaded) during ALL heavy loads in ALL populations. This is only the case if ALL populations are identified and then tested. Otherwise, this is limited at best to like-kind populations – populations with similar dysfunctions and pathologies, which is the general population.

Consider that one of the leading proponents for neck packing almost failed the Swing evolution at his RKC. This was because while trying to keep his neck packed, the natural happened – he was flexing his lumbar spine. When he actually did as we instructed him to do in the RKC / SFG – keep his eyes on the horizon – he was able to maintain the arch in his lower back. Surprise! You can't fight nature.

Nutrition Matters

Originally, when we wrote Becoming Bulletproof we included a section on nutrition. After all, nutrition certainly matters when it comes to growing strong and healthy. However, If we are being *completely* honest, we don't know <u>exactly</u> **how** it matters. What we mean to say is that nutrition is very important, if not extremely important to how well your body functions. However, there is SO much information out there - conflicting information where experts completely disagree on what to eat, when to eat, how to eat. Diving into all we "know" about nutrition can really drive a person crazy. The more you learn, the more you will end up chasing your tail.

For example, at the time we are writing this book, "Paleo" nutrition is popular: Low carb, natural whole foods, with an emphasis on meat and natural fats. It's supposed to be the "healthiest" way to live.

Except that when we were younger we lived off diets that were exactly the opposite - high sugar and high starch, combined with lots of running around and we were super lean.

So is there a difference in the metabolisms between growing kids and aging adults that make for such different and contradictory advice?

Consider this: When Geoff was 16 and a senior in high school, this is what his daily eating looked like:

630am: Drag self out of bed, 100 push ups, shower.

645-700am: 3-4 ounces of orange juice, 1 multivitamin

1045am: Mid morning break - 3 Musketeers candy bar + can of Cherry Coke

1150am - 1pm: Lunch - Meat hoagie, covered in mayo, chicken burger (deep fried and covered in mayo), french fries (and mayo), ice cream sandwich.

330pm - 530pm: Wrestling practice

630pm: Dinner - usually some sort of pasta and a "salad"

Weight: 158lbs. Bodyfat: Sub 10%.

Note: Lots of sugar, saturated fat, and starchy processed carbohydrates.

Now the naysayers will say, "yeah, but you were younger then and you were working out more."

True.

But at 40 he carries around an extra 30-40 pounds more muscle than he did then and is way stronger than he was then. He still trains 6 days a week, and is very active. Why can't he eat the same way as he did then? What is it that has changed, besides perhaps damaging (*ahem*, adapting) his metabolism to a low carb diet over a period of close to 10 years? Was it a change in movements? Lack of movement? Injuries? Movement compensations?

The answer is not as easy as it may appear to be. We know, we've checked.

Having said all that, we believe a few things about nutrition:

1. The body is made to thrive and not just survive. Yes, the body is great at adapting, but ideally, the body is made to thrive, to live. Low carb diets, no carb diets, and even paleo diets can put the body into "survival mode". While this may be fine for a season, it may not be fine for a lifetime.

2. We were made to move. And, we were made to eat. We should enjoy our food. If it tastes heavenly, that may be a good thing. If it taste like "bleck" maybe it is okay not to eat it. Life is made to be lived and therefore food is made to be enjoyed. Don't let food consume and imprison you.

3. Even though we said what we just said in #2, you can't expect to live off of Twinkies and Moon Pies if you want to look like Billy Beachbody, or Sally Swimsuit. Be honest with yourself and eat as well as you know how.

4. We were truly made to eat food - good tasting, nutritious food. We were not made to eat preservatives, additives, artificial sweeteners, Red Dye #66, or any other "natural" flavor, or almost safe chemical that you can think of. The closer your food is to the way God made it, the better off you probably are. Remember, we shouldn't try to outsmart our design. We are simply not that smart.

5. If there is a "good" food or a "bad" food, more often than not, you chose the label.

We know this section probably does not help you much. At best, this section is really just "food for thought." Nutrition is extremely important in regaining and keeping our original strength. But again, to be completely honest, we don't know what that "magic" formula is. We know we need carbs, we need protein and we need fat. We need salt, **we need sugar,** and we need sunlight. We don't need to live in the land of extremes when it comes to our food. Again, this may be another area where we should approach life as a child and eat good things (things that taste good) when we are hungry, sleep when we are tired, and play when we are awake.

What Do You Expect?

*I*f you are reading this book, we can only imagine that you are not satisfied with the thought of living with movement issues, injuries, "age related" issues, weakness, fatigue, apathy, or just insert any negative quality or issue here. You want more for yourself than just sitting around and watching life go by. You want to actually have "Golden Years" and not tarnished, brass years. In other words, you want to LIVE!

Here is a tough question for you: *What are you expecting?*

Are you expecting to be strong, healthy and resilient? Do you believe you will regain your original strength? Or, do you imagine yourself sick, weak, overweight, and lifeless? Another way to ask this is: When you "see" yourself in your mind's eye, what do you see?

The answer(s) to these questions is extremely important. You will become the way you think; you will get what you expect. If you believe you can regain the body you were meant to have, you will. If you believe you will end up in a rest home, you probably will. The thoughts you keep in your head get planted in your heart and they shape your beliefs, which in turn determines your outcome.

You might be thinking that we're getting all "spiritual" right now. And, you might be right. However, there is very much a physical truth to what we are saying here. Every single action you make, every single thought you have, actually changes the structure of your brain in order for your brain to become more efficient.[54] The brain strives for efficiency. When you have a thought, good or bad, a neural connection is made. This connection allows that thought to become more efficient. The more you think the same thought, the more you literally cement that thought into your brain.[55] Yes, it is true: Eventually it takes *less thought* to have that same thought! Remember, the brain operates on the "use it and keep it" principle. The more you entertain a thought, the more you cement the neural connection that was made by that thought, and the easier it is to have that thought. Your thoughts can become common to your brain. In other words, you can create *habitual* thoughts, good or bad. These habitual thoughts will eventually manifest themselves in your body, in your life.

This is one reason why it is imperative to control your thoughts and your imagination. When you see yourself in the future, you need to see yourself strong. You need to see yourself conquering mountains, climbing trees, sprinting down rabbits! You need to believe, to *know*, that you are capable and able to overcome obstacles. You need to see yourself ALIVE! If you are injured now, you need to know that soon, you will not be. Soon, you will be resilient. If you can't walk up a flight of stairs without gasping for air, you need to believe that you'll be bounding up those same stairs with ease in just a few short weeks.

Put good, positive thoughts - the images you want to become - inside of your head and keep them there. Think them over and over. Those thoughts will create habitual thoughts and end up shaping your beliefs. You know this to be true. Think of someone who always worries or who is always negative. Are they fun to be around? No, probably not. Now, think also on how those people act. Are they full of life and energy? No, probably not. Now think about how those people move and look. Do they move with strength and grace? Is their posture perfect? Or do they slump? Is their head protruded forward? Are their shoulders rounded forward as well? Yes, probably so.

Negative thoughts are "dead" thoughts. Dead things sink to the bottom of the lake, they decompose, they waste away. Positive thoughts are "alive", they have life in them. Things that are alive, rise to the top. They thrive.

Our thoughts present themselves in our bodies and our lives. We reflect how we think. If you want to be strong, if you want to have vitality, think strong! Think vitality, think LIFE! Remember, your thoughts actually change the physical shape of your brain. Thoughts become real, physical things! If you are going to change the shape of your brain, change it for the better. Expect health. Expect strength. Expect life!

And yes, this is also spiritual. Psalms 23:7 says, "For as he thinks in his heart, so is he." Simple wisdom makes for simple reality.

We know this may not be what you were expecting to find near the back of this book, but this could be the most important chapter of the whole book! If you want to regain your original strength, you need to think and believe that you will AND that it's easy to do. It is that simple.

The Magic Bullet

*I*s there a magic bullet to regaining your original strength and becoming bulletproof? Yes. Yes there is. There is one "magic" key to unlocking the body of your dreams - the body you were meant to have. **That key is simple consistency.** We know this was already touched on earlier, but we believe this topic bears repeating.

Simple consistency is the key to unlocking almost any goal.

Think about it. What is the best way to prevent cavities? By taking care of your teeth. And how do you do that? You brush them 2 to 3 times every day. **Every single day**.

The best plans in the world for any goal or endeavor will fail if consistent application is not applied. The best "diet" will not work if you do not consistently apply its principles. The best workout regimen ever invented will never produce the results it promises if it is not applied daily. You hold the keys to regaining your original strength, or any other goal that you hope for. You must consistently engage every single day; mentally if not physically. Though both are better.

"If it is important, do it everyday." - Dan John, who credits Dan Gable, wrestling phenom and legend. Those words are worth etching in your head with a permanent marker. If you want to unlock your full potential, you must engage daily. Whether it is your relationship with your spouse you want to improve, whether you want to lose 30 lbs, or you just want less cavities when you go to the dentist for your routine teeth cleaning, you must engage daily in the activities that will yield your desired outcome(s).

Jack Lalanne is a hero of Tim's. Jack is pretty much the father of fitness in this country as we know it. He died in 2012 at the age of 96 years old. At the age of 96, he had more energy, strength and stamina than most of today's 20-somethings do. He could still do finger tip pushups at 96 years old! How many of those can you do? You want to know what Jack's big secret was to his health and longevity? It was consistency. Every single day of his life, Jack exercised. Jack moved. Jack did something. He made a consistent effort to move his body everyday. And in his 90s he could still out work, out last and out perform most of this country's population. Jack knew the secret to a happy, healthy life. More than that, Jack took action and applied that secret to his **_daily_** lifestyle. Jack did something every day.

Did you catch Jack's secret to his health and success? It wasn't just his knowledge that made him healthy. It was the action that he took along with his knowledge. **_Action_ is movement**. Knowledge will only stay in your head if you do not act on what you know. Even if you do not know all that you need to know, if you act, you can make the knowledge you know work for you. In other words, action gets results. Consistent action gets lasting results.

Your body is simply awesomely made. You have everything you need to regain the original strength you were meant to have. All you have to do is engage, move, every single day. If only a little bit in the beginning; just take the first step, make the first roll, rock the first time. Then do it again tomorrow. You can do this.

Conclusion

*W*hen we decided to write this book and present this information, our only motives were to learn how to become as resilient as possible and to help others do the same. This is important to us because **we believe that a healthy, strong body leads to a healthy, happy life**.

There is a ton of great training information out there in the world. There are also many different schools of thought as well as various training systems out there. All of them have a lot of great information to offer. None of them are complete though. Not all of the training systems, or schools of thought, get along with each other. It is not our attempt to say that any-one's information is "wrong" or that our information is "right" or better than anyone else's training system. If anything, our goal is only to improve all training systems and modalities, to be *ambassadors*, if you will, to the other systems out there.

We honestly believe, and with good reason, that Original Strength is the foundation for life, health and longevity. It is the operating system, the foundation for anything you want to do or become. We believe it can enhance anyone's training modality. From Z- Health, to Functional Movement Systems, to kettlebell training, to Cross-Fit, to P90X - it doesn't matter how you want to train, or what system you want to use, we think our information presented here will make all other training systems better.

From Tim:

Aside from that, I have always wanted to be capable of physically doing anything. Basically, I have always wanted to be Superman. Yes, I am nearly 40 years old and I have never grown out of that fantasy. I used to think something was wrong with me until I read John Eldridge's book, *Wild at Heart.* I now think there is something wrong with everyone else who does not want to be Superman. Anyway, all of us, if we are being honest, have deep down inside wanted to be resilient, invincible, powerful, and strong. When Mike McNiff and I first put our ideas in *Becoming Bulletproof*, we thought we had found the secret to strength, health and resiliency. Now, as Geoff and I write *Original Strength*, I am certain that we have. The body is simply amazing. <u>It is wonderfully designed</u>. **We were made to be perfect.** We were made to move, to play, to live. Health is the key to being able to do all that you were designed to do. If all you want to do is just be a good parent, or volunteer at your local food shelter, or maybe you just want to be independent when you are 85, you need good health. What I mean is that if you truly want to enjoy your life to its fullest, you need to be as strong as you were meant to be.

Movement is the key to having good health. The more you move, the better your brain functions. The better your brain functions, the better you move. Movements, "resets", like the ones we have presented here are great tools for restoring our bodies' ability to move and function like they are meant to - perfectly.

I believe the information we have presented here is a great place to start for developing a fully functional, capable body. The *resets* in this book, if applied, can help you establish a **great foundation**, which is key to building a healthy structure.

As I said earlier, you have to put this information to the test. If you do not try anything in this book, you have no right to make any assumptions about what we are saying; good or bad. If you do desire to become more than you currently are, if you want to regain the strength you were meant to have, give yourself a few months to engage in this material. Rome wasn't built in a day. It took time and consistent effort to build one of the most amazing empires the world has ever known. So it is too with the body. ***Regaining your Original Strength is a journey***. Give yourself time to enjoy the journey.

You can do this. You can overcome weakness, apathy, complacency, injury, and anything else that is weighing you down or holding you back. You were meant to be strong, healthy, resilient, capable and able. You are fearfully and wonderfully made. You can regain the body you were meant to have. You were meant to live and enjoy this life. You were meant for great things. You were meant.

God bless.

From Geoff:

I have always wanted to be strong. I remember hanging from the clothesline at three years old trying to do pull ups. I'm not the strongest guy in the world by any means, but I'm not the weakest. And at 40 years old, in many ways I am stronger than I ever have been. I can do One Arm One Leg Push Ups, Pistols with weight in the rack, and I'm closing in on the One Arm Chin at a bodyweight of over 200lbs. None of those things could I do three years ago, nor at any other time in my life.

And after spending the last three years experimenting with the resets found in *Original Strength* - pulling them out of my training and putting them back in and comparing results, I can say definitively that this body of work underpins all strength efforts. It is the foundation for all strength. My clients' lives have borne this out. And our seminar participants are proving it both at the seminars and in follow up conversations.

Most importantly, I can keep up with my son, who is about to turn two. I get down on the ground, roll around, run, jump, crawl, and have a good ol' time with him. That's something that as little as five years ago wasn't even possible, not because we didn't have a child, but because I had a body that was broken - despite having spent tens of thousands of dollars on education to help me become "better than before."

Probably the best part about the Original Strength System is that anyone - *anyone* - regardless of age, background, or health history can do this stuff and greatly benefit from it with zero coaching except what they read in this book. In fact, you can do most of the resets in here "wrong" and still derive great benefit.

At the end of the day, this stuff is not only easy, it's fun. And isn't that part of life? Fun? Life is too short not to have fun. Especially with the ones you love.

So if pain and fear of injury and movement have been holding you back, I know how you feel. I've been there. I was "there" for a long time. Now I'm where I was supposed to be all along. It's like a form of restoration. You belong here too. The journey is actually surprisingly easy and enjoyable. I invite you come along. It's fun over here living where we are supposed to - in a world full of almost effortless movement. Hope to see you here.

Does your body remember how to do this? We are sure it does. Remember, regain, your Original Strength!

References

[1] Sally Goddard Blythe, *The Well Balanced Child* (Stroud: Hawthorne Press, 2005), p. xiv.

[2] Carla Hannaford, *Smart Moves* (Salt Lake City: Great River Books, 2005), p. 48.

[3] Carla Hannaford, *Smart Moves* (Salt Lake City: Great River Books, 2005), p. 32.

[4] Carla Hannaford, *Smart Moves* (Salt Lake City: Great River Books, 2005), p. 28.

[5] Sally Goddard Blythe, *The Well Balanced Child* (Stroud: Hawthorne Press, 2005), p. 176.

[6] Sally Goddard Blythe, *The Well Balanced Child* (Stroud: Hawthorne Press, 2005), p. 23.

[7] Barry Ross, *Underground Secrets to Faster Running* (BearPowered.com, 2005), p. 62.

[8] Carla Hannaford, *Smart Moves* (Salt Lake City: Great River Books, 2005), p. 111.

[9] Pavel Tsatsouline, Power to the People (St. Paul: DragonDoor Publications, 1999), p. 64.

[10] Carla Hannaford, *Smart Moves* (Salt Lake City: Great River Books, 2005), p. 38.

[11] Carla Hannaford, *Smart Moves* (Salt Lake City: Great River Books, 2005), p. 39.

[12] Idem.

[13] Sally Goddard Blythe, *The Well Balanced Child* (Stroud: Hawthorne Press, 2005), p. 13.

[14] Carla Hannaford, *Smart Moves* (Salt Lake City: Great River Books, 2005), p. 38.

[15] Sally Goddard Blythe, *Reflexes, Learning and Behavior* (Eugene: Fern Ridge Press, 2005), p. 20.

[16] Carla Hannaford, *Smart Moves* (Salt Lake City: Great River Books, 2005), p. 49.

[17] Sally Goddard Blythe, *Reflexes, Learning and Behavior* (Eugene: Fern Ridge Press, 2005), p. 59.

[18] Idem.

[19] Carla Hannaford, *Smart Moves* (Salt Lake City: Great River Books, 2005), p. 39.

[20] Sally Goddard Blythe, *The Well Balanced Child* (Stroud: Hawthorne Press, 2005), p. 18.

[21] Sally Goddard Blythe, *The Well Balanced Child* (Stroud: Hawthorne Press, 2005), p. 19.

[22] Idem.

[23] Carla Hannaford, *Smart Moves* (Salt Lake City: Great River Books, 2005), p. 111.

[24] Sally Goddard Blythe, *The Well Balanced Child* (Stroud: Hawthorne Press, 2005), p. 35.

[25] Carla Hannaford, *Smart Moves* (Salt Lake City: Great River Books, 2005), p. 91.

[26] Carla Hannaford, *Smart Moves* (Salt Lake City: Great River Books, 2005), p. 112.

[27] Carla Hannaford, *Smart Moves* (Salt Lake City: Great River Books, 2005), p. 131.

[28] Idem.

[29] Idem.

[30] Idem.

[31] Carla Hannaford, *Smart Moves* (Salt Lake City: Great River Books, 2005), p. 112.

[32] Idem.

[33] Idem.

[34] Sally Goddard Blythe, *The Well Balanced Child* (Stroud: Hawthorne Press, 2005), p. 185.

[35] Gray Cook, *Secrets of Primitive Patterns* (Functional Movement DVD series)

[36] Sally Goddard Blythe, *The Well Balanced Child* (Stroud: Hawthorne Press, 2005), p. 185.

[37] www.functionalmovement.com"

[38] Dan John, *Never Let Go* (Santa Cruz: On Target Publications, 2009), p. 123.

[39] Gray Cook, *Movement* (Santa Cruz: On Target Publications, 2010), pps. 187 - 189.

[40] www.functionalmovement.com

[41] Gray Cook, *Secrets of Primitive Patterns* (Functional Movement DVD series)

[42] http://www.sciencebuddies.org/science-fair-projects/project_ideas/MatlSci_p021.shtml

[43] Pavel Tsatsouline, *Power to the People* (St. Paul: Dragon Door Publications, 1999), p. 78.

[44] Pavel Tsatsouline, *Power to the People* (St. Paul: Dragon Door Publications, 1999), p. 79.

[45] Norman Doidge, *The Brain that Changes Itself* (New York: The Penguin Group, 2007), p. 208.

[46] http://en.wikipedia.org/wiki/SAID_principle

[47] Sally Goddard Blythe, *The Well Balanced Child* (Stroud: Hawthorne Press, 2005), p. 23.

[48] Norman Doidge, *The Brain that Changes Itself* (New York: The Penguin Group, 2007), p. 208.

[49] Sally Goddard Blythe, *The Well Balanced Child* (Stroud: Hawthorne Press, 2005), p. xiv.

[50] Tim Anderson and Mike McNiff, *Becoming Bulletproof* (Fuquay-Varina: Xulon Press, 2012), p. 60 - 63.

[51] Tim Anderson and Mike McNiff, *Becoming Bulletproof* (Fuquay-Varina: Xulon Press, 2012), p. 65.

[52] Bud Winter, www.budwinter.com

[53] http://en.wikipedia.org/wiki/Lloyd_(Bud)_Winter

[54] Norman Doidge, *The Brain that Changes Itself* (New York: The Penguin Group, 2007), p. xviii.

[55] Norman Doidge, *The Brain that Changes Itself* (New York: The Penguin Group, 2007), p. 209.

CPSIA information can be obtained at www.ICGtesting.com
Printed in the USA
BVOW021157290513

321878BV00011B/451/P